BUZZMARKETING

May The Buzz
Be with you !

BUZZMARKETING

get people
to talk about
your stuff

MARK HUGHES

PORTFOLIO

PORTFOLIO
Published by the Penguin Group
Penguin Group (USA) Inc., 375 Hudson Street, New York, New York 10014, U.S.A.
Penguin Group (Canada), 10 Alcorn Avenue, Toronto, Ontario, Canada, M4V 3B2
(a division of Pearson Penguin Canada Inc.)
Penguin Books Ltd, 80 Strand, London WC2R 0RL, England
Penguin Ireland, 25 St. Stephen's Green, Dublin 2, Ireland (a division of Penguin Books Ltd)
Penguin Books Australia Ltd, 250 Camberwell Road, Camberwell,
Victoria 3124, Australia (a division of Pearson Australia Group Pty Ltd)
Penguin Books India Pvt Ltd, 11 Community Centre, Panchsheel Park,
New Delhi–110 017, India
Penguin Group (NZ), Cnr Airborne and Rosedale Roads, Albany, Auckland 1310, New Zealand
(a division of Pearson New Zealand Ltd)
Penguin Books (South Africa) (Pty) Ltd, 24 Sturdee Avenue,
Rosebank, Johannesburg 2196, South Africa

Penguin Books Ltd, Registered Offices: 80 Strand, London WC2R 0RL, England

First published in 2005 by Portfolio, a member of Penguin Group (USA) Inc.

3   5   7   9   10   8   6   4

PUBLISHER'S NOTE.   This publication is designed to provide accurate and authoritative information in regard to the subject matter covered. It is sold with the understanding that the publisher is not engaged in rendering legal, accounting or other professional services. If you require legal advice or other expert assistance, you should seek the services of a competent professional.

LIBRARY OF CONGRESS CATALOGING IN PUBLICATION DATA
Hughes, Mark, 1965–
Buzzmarketing : get people to talk about your stuff / Mark Hughes.
p.   cm.
Includes bibliographical references and index.
ISBN 1-59184-092-9
1. Word-of-mouth advertising.   2. Publicity.   3. Mass media and business.   4. Marketing.
I. Title: Buzzmarketing.   II. Title.
HF5827.95.H84 2005
659.13'3—dc22   2004060233

Printed in the United States of America
Set in Adobe Life   Designed by Joy O'Meara

For Kathy

contents

introduction

Fasten your seat belt. You're about to experience some turbulence, because that's what happens when you leave the solid ground of convention behind.

You're about to dive into the world of buzzmarketing.

There's a lot of controversy being churned up about buzzmarketing. Most of what you hear or read on the subject is way off base. Critics say buzz is random, merely serendipitous, and can't be corralled, but those attacks come mainly from people who have never had their asses on the line—not as entrepreneurs, and not as people with something to lose. I've faced the gut-wrenching fear of knowing that forty people could be jobless if my marketing didn't work.

So this book isn't from a sideline player who's never really had skin in the game. I succeeded by harnessing the power of buzzmarketing. And I did it despite the warnings from traditional types who said it "couldn't be done that way."

When I spent $40 million a year on advertising in previous years, I marketed the way most everyone else does—by using major ad agencies and spending lavishly. The campaigns won some national awards, but they weren't buzzmarketing. Then I launched a start-up, and that's when I got buzz. Only when you've got *everything* to lose do you really understand the need to think differently. Without the fear of God, you tend to tread the familiar paths.

After playing the game both ways—big brands with big budgets and start-ups with cash-starved budgets—I found out the hard way that buzzmarketing works. It demands that you out-think instead of out-spend.

In this book you'll discover how some exciting but unfamiliar brands and some familiar ones (like Apple Computer, Pepsi, and Britney Spears) have used buzzmarketing to grow faster and expand further, and do it for one-tenth of what it costs by more traditional means.

I'll also share with you the Six Secrets of Buzzmarketing that will make it possible for you, too, if you want to grow faster, expand further, and do it smarter.

That's what you'll find in the following pages: the hands-on why, and the hands-on how, from someone who's succeeded by breathing it and doing it.

Fasten your seat belt, you're about to . . . *get buzzed.*

BUZZMARKETING

CHAPTER ONE

Evading the Stampede

When I worked in the corporate world of big brands, I spent millions of dollars on conventional advertising. And guess what I got?

I got conventional results.

As a big swingin' marketer with a big swingin' budget, I didn't incorporate much buzz into my marketing. I also didn't achieve *breakaway growth.* Yes, I won national awards and accolades, but a marketer with a big budget generally thinks he doesn't need buzz and misses out on possibilities for the kind of growth that makes executives and stockholders smile.

Only later, in the unleashed, dazzling world of hot start-ups, did I experience the newfound power to reinvent the wheel. In place of a big-bucks marketing budget, I used my creative instincts and had a blast doing it. The start-up world put me on stage and in the spotlight. My creative brain went full tilt into action. It was a great feeling, one shared by many savvy folks in those days before the bubble burst.

In the world of big marketing budgets, the pressures simply aren't the same. Sure, the marketing folks in a major company worry . . . but their worries have a different twist. Hey, there's always another marketing budget *next* year. In a start-up, everyone worries if there will *be* a next year. In a start-up, fear is built into the company DNA. For months I would go to sleep scared and wake up scared. We had to out-think versus out-spend. We had no choice. The only way we could grow profitably was with buzzmarketing.

Translation: Our marketing had to start conversations. Why? Because word of mouth is the most powerful form of marketing on earth. Period. Firms like Euro RSCG have documented the impact of word of mouth: ten times more effective than TV or print advertising. *Ten times* more effective. Yet many have no earthly idea how to trigger it.

I didn't, at first. Only by experiencing the two extremes of marketing budgets—big brands with big budgets, and start-ups with minibudgets—did I come to appreciate the value of buzz, and how it magnifies every marketing dollar. I saw firsthand how millions can be wasted by treading the path of conventional marketing, and I saw how marketing dollars can be stretched and multiplied by following the out-of-the-box route called buzzmarketing.

A big-time consulting firm might charge you $500,000 for a glimpse into the secrets of buzzmarketing. But you don't have to pay a ridiculous sum for someone else to get buzz going for your product or service. You can do it yourself. Keep reading.

What Is Buzzmarketing?

DEFINITION: Buzzmarketing captures the attention of consumers and the media to the point where talking about your brand or company becomes entertaining, fascinating, and newsworthy.

To put it simply: Buzz starts conversations.

In the traditional marketing model, the corporate marketer sits in the middle and spends money to send messages to targeted prospects. The marketing team creates a message, purchases media,

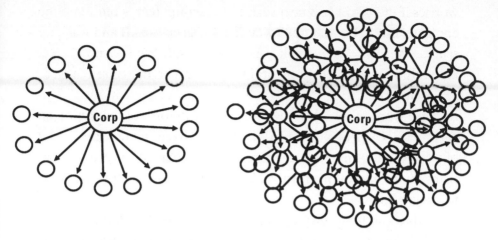

Traditional marketing model   Buzzmarketing model

and sees the messages delivered to the customer—whether business customer or consumer. End of story.

Buzzmarketing begins the same way: sending messages to consumers. Then it goes further. In the buzzmarketing model, the consumer tells two friends, those two tell two friends, and so on, and so on. Creating buzzzzzzz.

People tell others because you've given them something to talk about.

That's the essence, the key. If you haven't given people something clever, amusing, catchy, remarkable . . . if you haven't given them something they'll enjoy sharing with others to entertain, to sound smart or clever, to sound *with it*—forget it. You ain't got buzz.

You like to be around people who talk about stuff that's entertaining. Stuff that's fascinating. Stuff that's newsworthy. Giving people something to talk about is the only way buzzmarketing works.

Make no mistake, this takes creativity. But it's a creativity you can master, based on the principles in these pages. Buzzmarketing will propel your entire business and give it *staying power.*

Can You Afford Not to Be a Buzzmarketer?

Hoping to get noticed in the marketplace? The odds are dead set against you.

More than twenty-three thousand new products are introduced each year in America. Twenty-three thousand marketers and brand managers are competing for the same level of attention and the same purchaser's dollar. They all want to grow. They all want to achieve breakaway sales.

And those are just the *new* products.

What about brand products, and companies that already exist?

The real punchline...all these marketing execs think
they have your attention.

Take Motorola, Microsoft, McDonald's, Mentos, MasterCard, Mazda, Minolta, M&M's, Mercedes, Merrill Lynch, Michelob, Maybelline, Mitsubishi, Marlboro, Maxwell House, Mobil, Merck, MCI, MTV, Mizuno, Morgan Stanley, Marriott, Mattel, Milky Way, Maxim, Minute Maid, Maytag. What do they have in common?

All of these are fighting for attention—and that's just a list of *some* of the ones beginning with *M!*

Of every product introduced each year in the consumer packaged goods industry, 70 percent fail. Of all small businesses started in America, 80 percent fail within the first five years. Statistically, the odds are against you. But you're going to be the exception, because if you're reading this book, you're ready to listen, learn, and get buzz.

Debunking the Myths

Buzz has become a buzz word. And as happens with many buzz words, a cloud of confusion surrounds it. Let's set the record straight.

Buzzmarketing Is Not a *Means*

It is not akin to TV, or direct mail, or radio. Those are means. Those are vehicles. Buzzmarketing is about *ends.* Remember our buzzmarketing model schematic—you still have to send messages out to consumers. Those messages can be sent through a variety of methods. Nothing is off the table.

It might be solely word-of-mouth marketing; it might be complemented with TV, it might be complemented with radio, it might be complemented with a variety of media that could combine the traditional and the nontraditional. But the goal of a buzzmarketer with every dollar spent is: Spark further word of mouth. The real goal is to start conversations beyond the obvious message. It's all about getting people talking and the media writing about your brand. That must be the end you concentrate on.

Buzzmarketing Is Not "Guerrilla Marketing"

Guerrilla marketing may be a series of stunts (stickering, people dressed up in costume in major cities, etc.). It can be one of the means you utilize to send your message.

Buzzmarketing is something else: a way to get people talking and the media writing about your brand. Remember, buzzmarketing is all about the *ends.*

Sometimes buzzmarketing incorporates guerrilla marketing. But guerrilla marketing is one tool. You don't have to have it to get buzz. Britney Spears gets buzz—she uses zero guerrilla marketing. Don't confuse the two.

Companies like Procter & Gamble Do *Real* Marketing

Sure, it's tough to get over the logical notion that the giant firms, the companies that have been around for eons and own a humongous share of their market, must have the right answers about marketing. Stay with me. I'll have you convinced by the time you finish reading.

I can tell you that throughout my career I have been told, "You can't do it that way." And every time I prove them wrong. Buzzmarketing makes things possible. At Half.com, a well-heeled analyst from Chase Bank's capital group insisted that I couldn't grow Half.com to our target of 813,000 registered users in the first year. And he was right—I grew it to in excess of one million registered users in the first year. And over eight million in less than three years.

I've also had people tell me to learn the basics—to retake Marketing 101. I'm used to it by now. Interestingly, the best marketers get it. One key supporter of buzz, a man who helped inspire this book, was the chief marketer at a company that has been a marketing legend for one of the most famous brands in the world, one of America's leading soda companies.

He told me that thirty some-odd years ago he had the good luck to hang out with senior marketing execs at his previous company, Procter & Gamble. One day a senior exec told him what the two keys to success would be for him. First, "Ninety percent of your time will be wasted on stuff that doesn't matter, so do two or three colossal things really well each year." Second, "If you can ever figure out the secrets to word-of-mouth marketing, you've got it made."

Despite the naysayers, there are many people who get it, and not surprisingly they also happen to be way more successful than the naysayers.

Conventional experts will tell you that you'll need big ad budgets in order to experience breakaway sales growth. Bigger ad budgets equals bigger sales growth. Makes sense, right? Nope. The key is to outthink yourself, not outspend yourself. Outthink, not outspend.

Buzzmarketing Is Too Random

I never found buzz to be too random because the trick is to follow the structured, methodical approach to get people talking about your brand and to get the media writing about it.

Buzz is not a fad diet—it's a lifestyle change.

About This Book

I'm going to tackle buzz with you in two leaps.

First I'm going to open your eyes to the power of buzzmarketing by sharing dramatic examples of the best of the best. (Including, I modestly add, my own.) We'll also examine some cases in which successful products were not intrinsically different from the competition but enjoyed breakaway growth built on buzz.

Then I'll show you how to master the techniques these marketing powerhouses used and that I have used myself. You'll learn the Six Secrets that are the critical building blocks to creating killer buzz.

The Six Secrets are:

BUZZ BASICS
The First Secret—Push the Six Buttons of Buzz
The Second Secret—Capture Media
The Third Secret—Advertise for Attention

BUZZ LEADERSHIP
The Fourth Secret—Climb Buzz Everest
The Fifth Secret—Discover Creativity
The Sixth Secret—Police Your Product

That's what this book is about: How *they* got buzz. How *I* got buzz. And how *you* can get buzz.

Building a Brand on Buzz

Some brands, by all expectations, should have been creamed by competitors or, at very best, just muddled along. And yet they still managed breakaway growth. All the odds were against them—yet they came out of nowhere and shot ahead of the pack.

How did they do it, and how did I do it?

Read on.

CHAPTER TWO

Renaming a Town

You may be wondering what makes me an authority in buzzmarketing. It's time to share the story of how I and a few others put a start-up company on the nightly news and into newspapers all over the country. How I managed to grow our start-up, Half.com, from zero to eight million registered users in less than three wild, improbable years. There are those who might say that Half.com is just another dot-com success story that bubbled along with other dot-coms. But my story is relevant to today's market because it followed a path of growth by frugality instead of foolish expense or advertising convention. And it was all done with competitors nipping at our heels.

In 1999, I was the VP of marketing for this young start-up called Half.com, holding my breath along with a small staff as we waited for reports on efforts to raise the company's second round of venture financing. Nearly twenty competitors with similar business models lurked, some in hiding, some in plain view. It was dot-com fantasyland and everyone was trying to take the lead in our yet-to-be-defined category—an eBay-style virtual marketplace for buyers and sellers of books, movies, music, and video games (but with the retail look and feel of Amazon).

On my second day at the not-yet-launched company, the founder and CEO Josh Kopelman sat me down in his seven-by-seven-foot office in the old Lee Tire manufacturing plant. Launch was eight weeks away.

The CEO said to me, "One of the main reasons I hired you was for your background," and proceeded to rattle off some of my credentials. Then he told me, "You can throw all that out the window."

I sat there, bewildered, wondering where he was heading.

The mood in the venture capital community was shifting, he said. At this point, early in the dot-com bust, the venture capitalists (VCs) had witnessed the biggest waste of money in the history of marketing and advertising. *Their* money. VCs were becoming the least venturesome people around. An era was ending.

Josh laid it out plain and simple. Eighty percent of our money was going to be spent by *me* on marketing—and tradition simply wouldn't work in the cluttered environment of our industry. We had to come up with a Big Idea. An amazing idea. A marketing coup. And we had seven days to do it.

On the way out the door, he added, "No pressure!"

I think it was my first out-of-body experience.

What the hell had I gotten myself into? I'm a creative guy, yes. I'm a smart guy, yes. I achieved success by most standards, yes. I knew how to optimize a $40 million budget for improved marketing efficiency, but I never had to come up with an idea that could make or break a company. Thus began my ascent from thinking in the safe plane of corporate convention to a newer plane where turbulence was the goal. Creating a stir, creating buzz, and doing it with brains over bucks.

When I was at PepsiCo, the decisions and recommendations we made affected numbers on a spreadsheet—not people's livelihoods. Now, employees' paychecks depended on our success or failure.

Our CEO was employing the kind of creative leadership you'll read about in the Fifth Secret: Discover Creativity. He knew what 99 percent of CEOs don't—that consumers face a cluttered ad environment, so cluttered that most people simply don't pay attention to advertising. (CEOs—Are you paying attention here?)

He knew that conventional marketing would produce average results, and average was not going to get us where we needed to go. He demanded an entirely new kind of creativity and demanded the best.

The secret in all this is that demanding the best creativity forces you to think on a different plane—to be creative enough to devise an entirely new formula with a fraction of the budget of much bigger competitors.

Coming Up with the Big Idea

Clint Schmidt, one of my top marketing mavericks at Half.com, had been bird-dogging firms to help us come up with an idea powerful enough to save the day. We made a selection, hiring a firm that was the epitome of hip and what we thought was the epitome of buzz. Twenty-somethings dressed entirely in black. Almost too cool.

I felt uneasy. I could sense in the pit of my stomach that this firm didn't feel the pressure that Clint, myself, and others felt about our launch. Unlike us, every ounce of their creativity and energy wasn't dedicated to the cause.

The firm came to present their Big Idea. They launched into their pitch and gave us four ideas to choose from. One was a yard sale in Manhattan, and to be honest, I don't even remember the other three. My eyes met our CEO's, and we both knew if *these* were the Big Ideas . . . we were sunk.

We were out of time. I began brainstorming right there. The ideas rolled out one by one.

Mount Rushmore. Could we fly a helium balloon over George Washington in the shape of a cartoon-like thought balloon reading, "For rock-solid deals, head to Half."

The Hoover Dam. Could we shoot a zip wire across the dam with a huge banner hanging from it, reading, "Damn the high prices, head to Half.com." I began searching a virtual map in my mind for other national monuments.

And then it hit me. Among the thousands of towns across the country, surely there must be one town with the name Half in it. What better way to put the brand on the map than by literally putting the brand on the map. Let's find that Half town and convince them to change their name to Half.com!

I looked across the table to the folks from our not-helpful firm. They actually sneered at my idea and responded with an on-the-spot idea of their own: Slap our brand onto the recycling bins on the streets of New York. Oh yeah, that would get the media salivating.

Needless to say, we fired that firm shortly thereafter.

My colleagues and I knew we had the Big Idea now. But how do you get a town to change its name to Half.com?

Half Way to Halfway

As it turned out, there were many towns with Half in the name:

Half Acre, Alabama	Half Moon, Mississippi
Half Acre, New Jersey	Half Moon, North Carolina
Half Acre, Tennessee	Half Moon Bay, California
Half Bank Crossing, Oklahoma	Half Moon Landing, Georgia
Half Chance, Alabama	Half Moon Shores, Tennessee
Half Day, Illinois	Half Mound, Kansas
Half Falls, Pennsylvania	Halfa, Iowa
Half Hell, North Carolina	Halford, Kansas
Half Hollow, New York	Half Rock, Missouri
Half Moon, Arkansas	Halfville, Pennsylvania
Half Moon, Florida	Halfway, Arkansas

Halfway, Kentucky	Halfway, Virginia
Halfway, Louisiana	Halfway, West Virginia
Halfway, Maryland	Halfway, Wyoming
Halfway, Missouri	Halfway Creek, South Carolina
Halfway, New Mexico	Halfway House, California
Halfway, New York	Halfway House, Massachusetts
Halfway, Oregon	Halfway House, Pennsylvania
Halfway, Tennessee	Halfway Pond, Massachusetts
Halfway, Texas	

We liked the Oregon town because it was the smallest (population 350), and it was also near the Oregon Trail—the path of pioneers. We also liked Halfa, Iowa, because it would be amazing to say, "Halfa Iowa [half of Iowa] liked us so much, they renamed their town after us!"

We were forty-three days away from launching the site, so the pursuit began immediately. I called the town offices of Halfway, Oregon, hoping to speak to Mayor Ivan Richard Crowe.

Diana, the town secretary, answered the phone. She immediately spotted me for an outsider: Nobody calls him Ivan—he goes by Dick. "No, the mayor isn't in," she said. "But I'll take a message."

I left a message that I wanted to discuss marketing opportunities. I waited. Twenty-four hours passed. I called again. The secretary said she had given my message to the mayor, but he hadn't seemed too interested.

"I'm coming to California tomorrow and I'd like to stop by. Do you know if the mayor will be around then?" I said.

"Yes, there's a city council meeting tomorrow night. He'll be around."

"How do I get there from San Francisco?"

"Well, you should probably fly into Boise, Idaho. If you're renting a vehicle, you'll need a four-wheel-drive. This time of year, getting over the pass can be pretty difficult. Watch out for the deer. As you go over the final pass, you'll see Pine Valley, and you've never seen anything more beautiful. There's about two feet of snow on the ground. It's a four-hour drive from Boise. Good luck!"

On the long drive to Halfway, I called my dad to lay out how I was planning to rename the town. A Pulitzer prize–winning journalist, he also knew about small towns, an outcome of running small-town newspapers on Cape Cod after a life of national and international journalism. He chuckled, wished me good luck, but warned it would be an uphill battle. We both knew that small-town politics could be very divisive, and change wasn't always welcome. Nevertheless, my dad's laughter was supportive—because he thought the idea was truly crazy, yet he knew that if I could pull it off, the media wouldn't be able to get enough of it.

I descended into Pine Valley, and it lived up to the promise: It was beautiful, especially under two feet of fresh white snow. I stopped to take a picture of the town sign as a memento for my colleagues back at Half.

Driving into the center of town, I noted that Bryan's Sport Shop was selling guns and Birkenstocks. Interesting combination. Then came a quilt shop and a bank that looked as if it hadn't changed in ninety years. The Halfway Motel apparently doubled as the chamber of commerce. At the center of town was the small Pine Valley supermarket with a video rental store in front. Across the way was the Mercantile (a small version of Tractor Supply). At the center, the post office and Wild Bill's Bar & Restaurant. Fifty yards up, a chiropractor, barber, and the *Hells Canyon Journal*. A nine iron away, the Pine Valley Lodge and Olde Church Restaurant. No traffic lights.

Nickel-sized flakes of snow fell as I drove through the picturesque town—free of all big city life. I thought to myself, "There is no way I'm going to change the name of this place."

I found city hall, walked up to the lady at the desk and said, "Hi, I'm Mark Hughes from Philadelphia, you must be Diana."

"You actually came? I'll call the mayor and let him know you're here." She pressed a button on the phone and said, "Dick, that man from Philadelphia is here." Five minutes later, I met Mayor Dick Crowe. He stood before me—six-foot-five, solid barrel of a midsection, sweat on his brow, and wearing a baseball cap that had seen its share of hard labor. As he shook my hand, I noticed it was twice the size of mine and powerful enough to shame a Viking.

We sat and talked. I listened. I wondered. Ultimately, though, their goal for the town wasn't too far from ours. They wanted jobs, money, and a shot at improving their chance of growth (in their own stable way). Our goal was to put our brand on the map, and have a shot at improving our chance of growth (in a fast-paced way).

Now came the hard part. It isn't every day a stranger rides in asking a town to give up its name. Not only was this a challenge for me, but I had another handicap. A huge one. I couldn't tell the mayor what Half.com did. We were operating in what was called stealth mode because a good business plan could be stolen easily. We were operating in secrecy. Not only would I ask to take away the town's name and replace it with ours, I couldn't tell them what our name stood for.

I at last popped the question.

"What would you think about . . . perhaps changing the name of the town from Halfway to Half.com? Maybe, uh, just for a year?" I felt like a schoolboy asking my sixth-grade crush out on a date over the phone. Nervous. Short of breath. Afraid of rejection. Afraid of laughter. Yet praying that this relationship might have a glimmer of hope.

After an expectedly long pause, Mayor Crowe asked, "What's in it for us?"

I found a gasp of breath, and ran down a mental list—cash, ways to build the town a Web site and get local businesses online, the potential for hiring remote customer support people to provide jobs for the town.

We were two entities looking for new ways, alternative ways, and smart ways to grow.

The mayor stared. In a million years, he would have never expected someone to propose such a thing. Knowing there was a council meeting later that night, I asked if I could pitch the idea to the council.

And so I did. Much to my surprise and delight, I didn't get laughed out of town. The council asked questions. Sound, intelligent questions. Despite the fact that I couldn't tell them one iota about what Half.com did, I was beginning to think that maybe this looked promising. I asked the council to consider the idea, and made sure to mention that we had a list of other towns—like Halfa, Iowa—which would be competing against them. Since we were launching the Web site in January, we would need to know what their interest level was by December 15.

The mayor sized up the council members, as if seeking out naysayers. Then he looked at me and said, "I think we can get back to you by then."

I headed home, elated, feeling a strange sense of destiny.

All Hell Breaks Loose

About a week later, Josh called me and said, "I just got a call from the *Philadelphia Inquirer* asking what we're doing in a small Oregon town trying to rename it." Josh was not happy. "Mark," he said, "we want the media to pick this up at *launch,* not right now! How did this happen!?"

"I don't know. What did you tell the *Inquirer*?"

"I told them we'd give them the exclusive if they would sit on it until we launch in thirty days. The reporter said she'd get back to me in ten minutes. That was two minutes ago. We've got two choices: No comment, or we tell them what's going on, issue our own press release, and blow the whole story."

Tick, tock. Eight minutes.

"I know they had a council meeting last night. Let me call and find out what's going on."

I learned that according to the council minutes, the town had voted to rename the town. I was dumbstruck. I asked again to make sure I had heard correctly. Five minutes later, we decided to comment. We also wrote our own press release to ensure the Half.com side of the story was told, and sent it out over the general PR wire. But it was hitting newsrooms on a Saturday, probably the worst day to attract media attention.

Monday morning, my CEO called. I braced myself, not knowing how the conversation would go. It went well. Very well. We were making national news with a Town-Adopts-Company's-Name story. We were on *Good Morning America.* We were the front page story for *USAToday.com.* Radio stations, TV stations, and reporters were calling from all over America and from all over the world. That day, we would do more than forty interviews. And the press kept on coming. Buzzmarketing was putting the brand on the map.

All this . . . and we hadn't spent a dime on marketing or even signed a contract with the town. Not one dime.

Problems, Problems

As fate would have it, there had been a disconnect in communications at the council meeting. The tape machine recording the session somehow went dead, and the message from the town administrator was that the council had approved renaming the town, when in fact they had only approved moving forward to negotiate with us. This detail got lost in the press, and the townsfolk were pissed.

The mayor and the council assured residents no deal was done. But now a lot of hostility had built up and I sensed victory slipping away. I arrived in town hoping to salvage the deal amid a confused and angry population. Our proposal had opened a Pandora's box of small town politics and it wasn't pretty.

But press thrives on controversy. It worked to our advantage and gave us a leg up in the five most frequently written news stories (chapter 7, "The Second Secret—Capture Media").

I knew absolutely nothing about politics, but I drew upon a Harvard case study I had worked on at business school, called "Moving Ideas into Action: Mastering the Art of Change." One of the key lessons was influencing influencers. Mayor Crowe, as my guide, introduced me to all the influencers in town, one by one. I met with Julie, the bank manager; with the school principal; with Dale, the owner of the inn; John, the real estate mogul; Ira, the independent businessman making custom fly fishing rods. And with the Birkenstock store owner; the former doctor and largest rancher in the valley; the eighth-generation Nez Perce Indian who tended bar at Wild Bill's; and many more.

I shook a lot of hands and drank a lot of coffee. Most people were either suspicious or didn't like the idea. I kept on meeting, listening, and drinking more coffee. I simply tried to connect on a personal level. Just like a citizen of any small town, I sat with folks a while just to visit. A warm handshake and good listening were my only tools, but I hoped I was packing a little luck, as well.

A series of public hearings began; sparks flew, lightning bolts crackled, but the opinion leaders I had met with began supporting the town's renaming. In the course of meeting with these influencers, they learned the real facts, saw there was a human face to our company, and changed their mind about the whole renaming.

They began defending the idea calmly and then, in the face of opposition, moved into supporting it vehemently. It wasn't just *my* marketing coup . . . it became *their* marketing coup.

And this is the crux of buzzmarketing. Quintessential. Recall the two diagrams of ordinary marketing and buzzmarketing from the previous chapter. The traditional marketing model aims to send messages to people and, after those messages are delivered and the industry metrics of gross rating points calculated, the job is done.

Target met; marketing people go home. But the buzzmarketing model's sole purpose is to make your brand *their* brand. The sole purpose of buzzmarketing is to make your message so compelling, so entertaining, so fascinating, so newsworthy . . . that they want to tell more people—doing the marketing for you. Because the idea of the town renaming was a most fascinating, entertaining, and newsworthy event, it had this special buzz quality.

Once the influencers understood the facts and got the whole story, it became their cause. It became their buzz currency—not mine and not Half.com's. Buzzmarketing works only if you give other people currency—period. And I don't care if you're in one of the smallest towns in America or in one of the largest cities in America, renaming a town like this is a memorable event. Buzzmarketing isn't selfish. The crux of buzzmarketing is that it doesn't *grab* buzz currency . . . it *gives* buzz currency.

TV crews and reporters from AP, Reuters, and many newspapers began covering the public hearings, and the press snowballed on this small-town controversy.

People were beginning to take sides, and now was the time to play offense.

I shuttled back and forth between Philadelphia and Oregon. Half.com's Mark Harrington, Matt Jesson, and Clint Schmidt came out with me to meet more people and shake more hands. At 9:00 A.M., we met with the council members behind closed doors. We had them sign confidentiality agreements and then revealed the Half business model—letting the cat out of the bag.

Everyone in town knew the secret had been told to fifteen people, who were bound by silence. Naturally, the secrecy surrounding the concept was captivating (secrecy is detailed further in chapter 3). This was a critical element for us. The buzz built with even more momentum.

As we walked the streets of town, just about everyone stopped to talk. They wanted to get as close to the secret as possible.

Our whereabouts were known at every moment. Von Valcarcel, a renowned woodworking artist, put it colorfully: If we burped, everyone in town knew within three hours.

Then fifteen-year-old Brandi Wilson asked us to speak at her civics class at the regional high school, explaining that there was a lot of confusion about renaming the town among students and teachers.

At 1:00 P.M., we entered a civics classroom packed with students from several classes. With TV crews filming my every syllable, I told it like it was:

> *Yes, indeed, the name change is controversial. The reason why we were attracted to Halfway was because of its name. Changing the name of Springfield to Half.com wasn't interesting, but changing the name of Halfway to Half.com was novel and pressworthy.*
>
> *Yes, we were absolutely doing this to get publicity . . . putting our brand on the map. Shameless self-promotion.*
>
> *The financial part of the deal hasn't yet been finalized, but the renaming would only be for a year. The bipartisan committee would be the negotiating body, but the deal is looking like a combination of economic development funds, new computers for the elementary school, and a Web site for the town—totaling over $100,000.*

We were peppered with questions, but most important, the students saw we were real people and our intentions were up front.

At the end of the hour, we broke out two hundred Half.com T-shirts we had sent along in advance . . . not knowing how, when, or why we might use them. That day, nearly every high school kid went home wearing T-shirts that no one else in town had.

We had given them unrestricted access to us for more time than almost anyone else in town. They had had a chance to skewer me any which way they wanted. And at the end of the day, they had gone home with the buzz currency of a T-shirt that symbolized exclusivity. Most of those students told their parents these guys were cool. Those students turned out to be our biggest influencers. They had more information than their parents, and they saw us for what we were with their own eyes.

We were honest, we were up front, we were open, and we talked in everyday language. We were 100 percent the opposite of most marketing and advertising today, that usually tries to put *on* the polish, *disguise* the warts, and use corporate-speak like "new and improved." Most marketing today isn't honest and open. Guess what, consumers aren't dumb, and they see it for what it is: bullshit.

The tide was going our way. But another storm was coming to beat us back.

It all looked great. *New York Times* reporter Sam Howe Verhovek wrote a long article on the proposed name change. The story was scheduled to run on the front page of the *Times,* but news of the AOL Time Warner merger broke and bumped us to the National Report section. The story included my David and Goliath quote saying that Half.com would be "the most exciting site since Amazon or eBay."

The *Wall Street Journal,* the Associated Press, and even the *South China News* ran the story. NBC's *Today* show wanted an exclusive, and we negotiated to give them the interview the day the site launched. Getting the *Today* exclusive was a coup, but it only added excruciating pressure to win the town.

Then things turned for the worse. An opposition group had formed and began an organized effort to dismantle the renaming.

All the confidence drained out of my body. But in a matter of minutes, the town influencers began mobilizing people to fight the opposition. I was stunned. It was as if we were in the Wild West. The bad guys were coming, and the posse would meet at city hall at high noon.

Volunteers were mobilized. Twenty people were split up into

teams of two, delivering a two-page fact sheet door to door, to every house in the valley. The fact sheet also invited everyone to a public hearing. Five hours later, the handouts were all distributed. Now we waited.

At 8:00 P.M. the next night, the hearing began. It was the largest public meeting the town had ever had, and went on for three hours. Passionate pleas were made, sparks flew, and the deputy sheriff, armed with his pistol, was called on the scene in case things turned physical. The opposition called for a referendum, only to be denied. The council would have the final vote. Upon suggestion, they took a nonbinding poll: 75 percent favored the name change, 25 percent were against. The council approved renaming the town Half.com.

At 7:34 A.M. the next morning, Katie Couric began a five-minute segment with our CEO and the mayor. The site had gone live just hours before (a bit too close for comfort), and our brand was on the map—*literally*.

Recap

The Half.com story is an ass-on-the-line experience that embodies most of the Six Secrets of Buzzmarketing. It's a story of ascending to a higher plane of thinking by demanding creativity. Business managers and marketers with great skills can achieve explosive growth . . . if they demand creativity, encourage creativity, and do so with no holds barred. If you allow yourself, you will find explosive growth by shifting from the traditional model to a buzzmarketing model. Yes, it will seem unfamiliar. Yes, you will be criticized. And yes, it will work.

Quite often, buzzmarketing ain't sexy. It's unglamorous and uncharted territory for most CEOs, managers, and marketers. Tell your boss you'll be away for the next six weeks trying to rename a town . . . and you're likely to get fired. But you could also get rich.

The effort involved can be enormous. But so can the rewards for your business.

Before we had spent a single dime in traditional marketing, we had captured the attention of the media and the Internet community. *Time* magazine called it "one of the greatest publicity coups" in history. We created buzz, and we defined an entire category.

And twenty days after our launch, eBay called.

Within six months, we sold the company to eBay. The price tag was $300 million.

Moving forward with our buzzmarketing philosophy, we catapulted to the top ten list as one of the most trafficked retail sites on the Internet in less than a year, with budgets one-tenth the size of our competitors.

In less than three years, I grew Half.com from zero to eight million registered users.

So ask yourself—do you want to send messages out to people, and that's it?

It'll cost you a lot of money, and you may have very little to show for it. A better solution is getting buzz—devoting every ounce of effort toward getting people to talk about your brand and the media writing about your brand.

The Half.com story embodies most of the Six Secrets of Buzzmarketing. Let's look at them more closely so you can start using them right away.

CHAPTER THREE

The First Secret—
Push the Six Buttons of Buzz

What is great marketing? Aaahh, yes—identifying the holy grail.

This is the question many CEOs and small business owners ask over and over: "How can we bring great marketing to our company and break out our brand?" A marketer's typical response is, "Let's look at some of the best marketers of all time and duplicate what *they* did."

Follow this line and what happens next? You read articles. You interview professors. You find yourself looking for respected brands and may very well come up with Procter & Gamble as the model to examine.

You discover that Procter & Gamble tests their TV commercials rigorously in focus groups. And before producing their final commercials, they test first draft versions (called animatics) for persuasion scores. They test intensity levels of media for these commercials.

And maybe, like many others before, you decide that you've discovered the secret to great marketing. They wrote the book on marketing, right? Just duplicate what Procter & Gamble does, right?

Sorry. It won't work.

Why? Chances are you don't have Procter & Gamble's billions of advertising dollars and resources at your disposal. Furthermore,

Procter & Gamble hasn't created buzz in a *long* while. They've been focused more on refining than reinventing.

What's the Secret?

One of the secrets to word of mouth is that you're speaking face-to-face, which gives you what tons of marketers are trying to get every day: attention. Face-to-face attention competes with no other media, grabbing undivided mind share.

Another secret to word of mouth is credibility. When your friend, a neighbor, a coworker, or a family member tells you about a great movie, product, or service, you believe them. They're not being paid to pitch the item and so you give them full credibility. That's why having a great product matters so much: If you can wow 'em, people *will* tell their friends and neighbors.

In addition to face-to-face attention, audio stimulus stays with you longer, providing superior memory retrieval. In a study of two groups, only 49 percent of people recalled advertising based on a visual cue, while 70 percent recalled advertising from a thirty-second musical cue. Given the right context of attention, audio stimuli can be far superior to visual.

Why It Matters More Than Ever

Why should you care? Not only is word of mouth ten times more effective than print or TV, word of mouth is more important *today* than at any time in the past, for four reasons:

1. The ad clutter is rising to intolerable levels in America (a 283 index on the Clutter Curve; see chapter 10).
2. Traditional forms of media are rising in cost, compounding the issue of clutter.

3. We've been lied to so many times with advertising, it seems like the only message we trust these days comes from regular people like you and me.
4. Technology is accelerating word of mouth.

Because of technology, word of mouth is moving faster than ever before. Text messaging, e-mail distribution lists, chat rooms, message boards, Web sites, and blogs. If you see a great movie—bam, you're sending an e-mail to sixty-three of your friends in an instant and you have the buzz currency of being in the know. If the movie stinks—bam, an e-mail goes out to those sixty-three friends warning them to save their money. You become the hero for saving all your good buddies $20 for a pair of tickets and popcorn. With BlackBerrys, Treos, Pocket PCs, WiFi, and WiMax, we don't need to be tied to a desktop computer. We've got mobile communication with us for instantaneous messaging.

Most important, though, word of mouth used to travel in unique settings where a conversation could never be heard again. Now, with the Internet, a permanent history of word of mouth stays recorded *forever.* Bad or good, the Internet has transformed word of mouth from a single-engine dogfighter to an F-16. It's now become fast, powerful, long-range, and dangerous if you can't harness it. It can be your biggest asset in today's marketing world, or it can be your biggest nightmare if you can't control it.

But it's so simple to say, "Just start a word-of-mouth marketing campaign." Obviously it's not that simple do to. Flying this powerful machine requires knowledge, patience, and deliberation. Hang on.

Basic Training

The entire crux of word-of-mouth marketing is giving people a great story to tell.

Why? Because most of us love to be the center of attention; we love to have something interesting, amusing, or novel to talk about, something others will find entertaining, fun to hear . . . and will remember us for having brightened their day a little. Remember our definition of buzz:

Captures the attention of consumers and the media to the point where talking about your brand or company becomes entertaining, fascinating, and newsworthy.

A conversation starter. You've got to give 'em something to talk about because most of our products and services are simply boring. Law firm—boring. Exterminator—boring. Green beans—boring. Office supplies—boring. Computers—boring. Boring, boring, boring.

If you want people to talk about your product, you've got to give them a reason to talk about your product. Give them a story, and not just any story.

Take yourself back in time to 1984. On the day after the Super Bowl, can you imagine people talking about a computer? Watercooler conversation centered around MIPS or DRAM? Absolutely not. Boooorrring! Apple Computer got everyone in America talking about its computer because it gave people a story to talk about.

Not the product, not its attributes. People talked about that amazing commercial, about the audacity of poking IBM in the chest, about George Orwell's book *Nineteen Eighty-Four,* about the new era of Big Brother and how there might be a minimicrophone recording their every word at the watercooler right then and there. The story is not Apple's technology, all its MIPS and DRAM crap, but Apple is at the center of the story, and Apple is the giver of buzz, allowing people to tell a story to their coworkers and neighbors.

A buzzmarketer's dream is to start conversations that begin

with phrases like "You're never gonna believe . . ." and "Hey, did you hear . . ." Yet within the context of these conversations, their brand rests at the center. The giver of buzz.

The membrane of word-of-mouth marketing is that people love to tell stories—ever since the *Odyssey* and before, all the way back to the first tribal storytellers, the human race has been a culture around the spoken word, revering the elder who could grasp the attention of a circle of listeners and hold them spellbound.

Remember Bonnie Raitt's song, "Let's give 'em something to talk about"? You've got to do the same thing. Give 'em a reason to talk about your brand. What you've got to do is create a ready-made story for watercooler conversation.

We did this with Half.com. It wasn't an especially exciting product. Talking about a Web site that sold used and overstock books, CDs, and DVDs isn't exactly titillating—there were competitors in the marketplace doing the same thing, and no one was talking about them.

We had to give people a reason to talk about our brand. We had to give them a ready-made story. Renaming a town from Halfway to Half.com gave the world a great story to tell, and it propelled us from a no-name Web site to a top ten retail site in less than six months. The better the story, the faster the spread of word of mouth.

We talk about things that make us gasp, things that make us laugh, things that make us wonder, things that make us marvel. We talk about things that shock us, and things that thrill us.

But why do we talk about these things?

On the surface, we talk about them because they're emotive and they're interesting.

But dig a bit further into the human psyche and you'll discover we talk about these things because we want to be the center of interest. Imagine you're at a cocktail party. Introducing interesting news gives you a certain currency. For example, being the first one to discover an unknown gem of a restaurant gives you currency. Introducing entertaining and fascinating news makes you entertaining and fascinating.

And after all, who doesn't want to be entertaining and fascinating?

You've got to give 'em something to talk about—because it makes *them* interesting, and it gives *them* currency. Hey, Mr. Motorola and Miss Minolta, it's not about you . . . it's about them! If you don't create a story that gives *them* currency . . . word of mouth will not spread.

So you're well on your way in basic training. There are a lot of buttons in the F-16 of buzz, but there are six magic buttons to push that produce currency and start conversations.

They're tried and true. I call them the Six Buttons of Buzz.

Push the Six Buttons of Buzz to Start a Conversation

Creating buzz sounds very tough. But it can be easy if you know which buttons to push.

Time and time again, these six things push people's buttons and start conversations:

THE SIX BUTTONS OF BUZZ
- The taboo (sex, lies, bathroom humor)
- The unusual
- The outrageous
- The hilarious
- The remarkable
- The secrets (both kept and revealed)

Push any one of these buzz buttons, and you'll give people the currency to start a conversation.

Maxim 1: Push the Taboo Button to Start Conversations

Even Procter & Gamble stumbled upon taboo many years ago with Mr. Whipple and his admonishment, "Don't squeeze the Charmin!" Whipple told America it wasn't allowed in the store . . . we couldn't squeeze the Charmin. And the Mr. Whipple campaign was the most successful campaign in the brand's history. Time after time, a Procter & Gamble ad agency would try to kill off Whipple and replace him with a new campaign—only to return to Whipple, because sales were higher with Whipple. Whipple succeeded because he tapped into our taboo. When we arrived at the supermarket aisle for bathroom tissue—what did we do? Squeeze the darn Charmin, of course! Why? Because we knew we weren't supposed to do it—it was taboo.

Why did our urinal screens work for Half.com ("The Third Secret," detailed in chapter 10)? First, because it suggested a contextual message that was creative (Don't piss away half your money . . . head to Half.com). But second, because it was bathroom humor.

Bathroom humor is taboo—and we talk about the taboo. If you're ever at a dinner party with parents of babies or toddlers, give yourself thirty minutes before somebody starts talking about doo-doo and diapers. Of course you're not supposed to talk about those things at a dinner party—they're taboo. Or Viagra—can you imagine your parents or grandparents talking about bedroom performance except when alone in the bedroom?

Got a boring product like shampoo? Introduce taboo. Herbal Essences did. Each commercial pictures a woman in the shower, orgasming in sheer delight as she washes her hair with Herbal Essences shampoo.

Clairol turned a humdrum Herbal Essences "organic" into an industry star with their vibrant commercials playing on the close wording of *organic* and *orgasmic*. Every time you see their commercial, you see playful (but taboo) images of women enjoying their shampoo . . . as much as an orgasm.

Just think if GM's Hummer could get Hugh Grant in one of its commercials (unconsciously reminding us how he was caught by the police for, er, getting a hummer from a lady of the evening). Talk about taboo! That would get the whole world talking!

Maxim 2: Push the Unusual Button to Start Conversations

David Letterman's got the unusual buzz button nailed with his "Stupid Human Tricks" and his "Top Ten" lists. For marketers, look as far as Pepsi's decision to put a competing product, Coke, in the Pepsi Challenge commercials (revolutionary in its day, and still not done much today). Unusual marketing makes its way into pop culture and gives people currency.

In a very different kind of business, a man named Ian Klein decided to go into the online dating business five years ago. But when you're competing against Match.com, things get pretty competitive. His sister was one of the 64 percent of overweight Americans, and also one of the eighty million single people in America. In time, he made the connection, pushed an unusual button, and created a niche site called OverweightDate.com. Among overweight singles, the whispers started: at Weight Watchers meetings, at bars, everywhere.

Best of all, the idea worked. People who had been shelling out $40 a month on Match.com and getting zero dates because of their weight were now getting dates left and right. These days when founder Ian Klein walks through the mall in the Boston area where the site is based, people stop him to ask about it. If he'd put on a T-shirt with the OverweightDate.com name, he'd get stopped even more.

Will he resort to having fliers slipped to people eating at In-N-Out Burger locations in California? You bet. They're handed to everyone—overweight people, athletic people, skinny people. People laugh, they actually read the flier, and most important of all—they talk. It becomes an unusual conversation piece.

With marketing held to word of mouth, fliers at In-N-Out Burgers, some keyword buys online, and a few T-shirts, OverweightDate.com's registered user count tallies in the millions. Push the unusual button.

Maxim 3: Push the Outrageous Button to Start Conversations

You can't get more outrageous than asking a town to rename itself. Still, the town went for it.

But a word to the wise when you push this button. Outrageousness for the sake of pure outrageousness doesn't resonate too well. If you try to get attention by shooting gerbils out of a cannon (as Beyond.com did), that's certainly outrageous. But if you push this button just for the sake of being outrageous, it will probably work—giving people something to talk about. But what's the connection to your brand or product?

There needs to be *some* connection. In renaming our town, the *half* connection was obvious to everyone—and plenty of people found it outrageous. What you'll find with an idea that's too outrageous is that people might remember the ad but not the advertiser . . . unless there is a connection. (The gerbils probably didn't do much for Beyond.com, even if people remembered and talked about the ad.)

Here's the difference. A hypothetical situation: a porn star in the GM Hummer commercial. Outrageous? Yes. Any connection? *No.* So—a bad decision.

Now let's put Hugh Grant in a GM Hummer commercial. Outrageous? Yes (and taboo). Is there a connection? *Yes.* A good decision? Debatable.

The point is: The outrageous button will always work. It just works ten times better if there's a connection between your product and the outrageousness.

Maxim 4: Push the Hilarious Button to Start Conversations

The hilarious button works, but it may be one of the harder buttons to push—being truly funny is never easy. It can work to your advantage if done right, and to your disadvantage if you're on the wrong end of it.

A client of ours, the foods and household products company Reckitt Benckiser (they sell nine million household and personal care products every day) came to us with one of its tougher challenges. The brand was French's Potato Sticks, and it was a classic case of milking the profits with not much marketing spend. As a test, they asked what we could do. The budget wasn't huge, and we weren't sure if we would even accept the project, but off I went to the grocery store for three hours one night to make my decision.

The baseline situation was awful. French's Potato Sticks used to be sold in a can but the company had recently started putting it in a stand-up pouch. It reduced the visibility of the product, but the cost savings of switching to a pouch were too attractive to pass up.

The positioning in the grocery aisle was awful, too. Right next to Pringles, but low down on the shelf. Hard to see, hard to find, more competitors from the Doritos family arriving. A recipe for disaster, but it was a small cash cow. I lurked in the aisle and asked everyone who walked by if they knew about Potato Sticks (making clear I was a marketing and PR person, not a wacko). Nearly every person paused, squinted, and seemed to reach into the recesses of their brain and said, "Yeah, I used to have them as a kid." Bingo.

It wasn't so bad after all. All it took was a prompt . . . a conversation . . . and people remembered.

The next day we called to take on the project. I didn't know what we were going to do, but I knew if we could spark some word-of-mouth conversation, it would be easy to recall a brand people knew when they were kids. We later presented a two-week, intensive campaign that focused on nostalgia and comedy.

We would literally bring Potato Sticks to life—with comedians. We recruited amateur comedians and gave them the exposure and the prayer (long shot) of getting on *The Ellen DeGeneres Show* or *The Tonight Show*. Each day, we would have three comedians show up in Potato Sticks costumes that looked like your eight-year-old made them. Talk about rough around the edges, these were made from U-Haul cardboard boxes and spray paint. When passersby saw these people in costumes, they couldn't help but stop, approach, laugh, and ask, "What the heck . . . ?"

Purposefully, we designed the costumes to look homemade rather than corporate. The costume begged inquiry. They were our conversation openers. But once you start a conversation, you've got to continue it, make people laugh (in this case) and give them a ready-made story to take away with them and talk to other people about.

The comedians had no problem making people laugh—office workers, cabbies, teenagers, tourists, gays, straights, hot chicks, metrosexuals, old ladies, cops, and suits . . . they all stopped, listened, and laughed. Along with a product sample to eat, the punch line was, "Potato Sticks . . . they're back!"

Combined with two weeks of appearances all over Boston, and a Web site with riddles to guess the next Boston location, these comedians gave out twelve thousand packages of Potato Sticks.

Since this was a test, Reckitt Benckiser wanted to measure awareness results as well as sales. They spent $15,000 on the awareness study, and to be honest, we were nervous about the results of the study even though we were confident the plan would work. We were pushing the hilarious button, it was planned extremely carefully and deliberately, with locations chosen to cross-pollinate throughout the Boston metro area.

Before our campaign, unaided awareness of French's Potato Sticks tallied a mere 10 percent. With three comedians and twelve thousand packs of Potato Sticks—unaided awareness in the Boston metro area more than doubled from 10 percent to 21 percent.

If you know anything about awareness statistics, they are like glaciers. It takes eons to move them. What we had done was start conversations and make connections. We pushed the hilarious button to do it. Humor isn't easy, but when it works, it works well. We weren't just getting exposure and impressions. We made people laugh. They took pictures of our comedians, and our comedians took pictures of them. The entire purpose was not to sell, but to give. Give people something to laugh about . . . and a ready-made story to talk about.

Maxim 5: Push the Remarkable Button to Start Conversations

How do you make auto parts worth talking about, among people who ordinarily wouldn't? When I ran marketing and advertising for Pep Boys, we looked at all the categories that moved the needle in our business and picked a few "leader" categories to promote. One of these categories was brakes. Whether you're a do-it-yourselfer or prefer to have a mechanic fix your brakes, you need reliable brakes. Everybody does.

So how do you create advertising about brakes that starts conversations and gets people remarking on brakes? First, we had a creative team at our ad agency, DDB, that produced a great commercial. It opened up with two guys driving back from a weekend in the mountains clad in plaid shirts. They're driving their Ford Explorer along a winding mountain road as country music plays on the radio. They pass a moose-crossing sign . . . then another sign labeled REALLY BIG ONES. Looking at each other bemused, they continue driving. They pass another moose crossing sign labeled NO KIDDING. They now look at each other confused, then immediately jam on the brakes—stopping just short of a huge moose, standing twelve inches in front of their vehicle. The moose calmly looks at the drivers . . . and begins to speak.

"Hey, did you get them brakes at Pep Boys?" says the moose.

The camera cuts to the two guys—shocked by the talking moose. The driver responds in bewilderment, "Yeah . . . I did."

The unscathed moose then responds, "I appreciate it," followed by a closing promotion on brakes at an attractive price point.

The commercial itself was very good and bordered on the type of marketing that people would talk about. But we needed a boost. So to enhance the word of mouth and get people remarking on it, we created an in-store campaign with the moose. Tapes of the moose commercial were sent to all the stores, and the employees loved it.

We then had employees in every store wear a round button with a picture of the moose saying, "Ask me about Raybestos brakes." And guess what? When a customer sees a moose button on your shirt with an "Ask me about . . ." they remark "What's up with the moose?" It started conversations between customers and the sales associates.

It also started a conversation among employees. They talked about the commercial, and they also talked about the new line of Raybestos brakes promoted on the button. So when customers asked about the brakes, employees knew the features and benefits and were prepared to make the sale.

Based on the expected trend of sales from the prior year, brakes showed a double-digit net increase. The commercial itself was very good. But what pushed it over the edge was the in-store campaign causing employees and customers to talk about this crazy moose. We created a campaign that would push people's buttons and start conversations.

Maxim 6: Push the Secrets Button to Start Conversations

How many times has someone said to you, "I'm not supposed to tell you this, but . . ."

Secrets are currency. Revealing a secret is a definite conversation starter. People love to talk about secrets, and when they do, they become "in the know." They become part of an exclusive circle, and exclusivity is the cousin of secrecy.

Sometimes withholding can work better than flooding. Limit supply and everybody's interested. Limit those in the know of a secret, those not in the know want the currency of knowing—they want to be part of the exclusive circle. Withholding a secret can push people's buzz buttons, and get people talking.

While not intentional, Google's Gmail created secrecy and exclusivity in its Gmail account. At one point, people were paying $200 on eBay for an account (I admit I paid for one on eBay myself). But the crazy thing is . . . it's a lousy e-mail account (yes, it does have one gig of storage . . . perhaps enough for twenty years of one person's e-mail archives). But you can get e-mail accounts anywhere.

Although it's standard practice in the world of technology to create a very small list of beta test users, Gmail was kept a secret. It became exclusive to have an address like *Joe@gmail.com*. Limit supply, create exclusivity, know the secret, and more people want to know also. They get interested in what they can't readily have, and people talk. Shhh . . . push the secret button.

Who's Got Marketing Power?

Do brands with big budgets have marketing power? Maybe.

The brands with real marketing power are the ones pushing the Six Buttons of Buzz—and letting word of mouth proliferate exponentially. When consumers start talking, they begin marketing your brand for you.

Word-of-mouth marketing works well because of attention. When people talk to each other, they've got undivided, face-to-face attention—something conventional advertising rarely achieves. Word-of-mouth marketing also succeeds because of credibility. When an advertisement tells us to buy a product, we know it to be biased; we know it to be advocacy. When our friends and family members tell us about a great product, we believe them.

Big brands and small start-ups using word-of-mouth marketing achieve three to ten times higher sales than traditional marketing. George Lois, who put Tommy Hilfiger on the map, puts it at the top end of that range, claiming a ten-times impact when you create buzz.

But remember, word-of-mouth marketing ain't easy. You've got to create a story . . . ready-made for watercooler conversation. It's got to be entertaining, fascinating, and newsworthy. You've got to give 'em something to talk about. Connections count, impressions don't.

When people begin talking about your brand, you'll break away from the pack in no time. Push people's buttons—the Six Buttons of Buzz.

Recap

Can you reach far more people with one TV ad than with word-of-mouth marketing?

If you call impressions meaningful, yes. If you're talking about consumer connection—people who actually pay attention to you—not in a million years.

Word-of-mouth marketing isn't about you and your brand. It's about them—the people who will start the conversation for you. You have to be a buzz giver—creating a ready-made story to make *them* the center of interest.

Push the Six Buttons of Buzz. They're tried and true:

- The taboo (sex, lies, bathroom humor)
- The unusual
- The outrageous
- The hilarious
- The remarkable
- The secrets (both kept and revealed)

Are people really that easy to figure out? Aren't we much more involved and more intricate as human beings? Of course we are. We read books. We talk about philosophy. We all seek a deeper level.

But at the same time, we want to be entertained, and we want to entertain others. There's nothing new about this. The playwrights of the ancient Greek comedies understood about entertaining to hold people's attention; Shakespeare understood it. Buzz and word of mouth are just as predictable.

Give people currency, give them entertainment, and discover an explosion about to happen with your brand.

CHAPTER FOUR

Miller Lite: A Brand Before Its Time

So if you're a big brand launching a product without a defined category, how do you do it? How does a big brand get people talking?

Miller Lite was just that. A brand before its time. On the surface, it didn't have a chance.

In the 1970s, the market share for low-calorie brands tallied a minuscule 0.3 percent of all beer consumed. Heavy beer drinkers (that means people who drink heavily, not Mr. Beergut) accounted for 85 percent of the consumption, and they didn't want a low-calorie beer. It was considered sissy.

Several low-calorie brands attempted to capture the market, only to fail one after the other. Piels introduced Trommer's Red Letter in 1964 and yanked it off the shelves within weeks because of lousy sales. Rheingold introduced Gablinger's in 1967, and it also faltered. Others, too, littered the beer industry's low-calorie cemetery. There just didn't seem to be a market for light beer.

Despite the soggy track record of others, in 1973, the Miller Brewing Company of Milwaukee decided to dive into the market with a brand called Lite. Given the track record of other attempts, it should have failed as well. But ten years later, Miller Lite ranked as the number two selling beer in America, second only to Bud-weiser.

So what happened?

Sure, they started with the essentials—a great product, great consumer insights, and courageous decision making. But they managed to conceive an advertising approach that created a buzz. People talked about those commercials—creating buzz for nineteen years.

Before Lite was launched, however, Miller wasn't the power-house we know today. It was merely one-third the size of Bud-weiser, and ranked down at number six among all beer companies in America. At the time, Miller was selling its lead brand, High Life, as "The Champagne of Bottled Beer," even though 80 percent of beer was consumed by blue collar workers—not exactly the champagne crowd. In 1969, Philip Morris bought Miller Brewing Company; the new owners envisioned repositioning Miller High Life to heavy beer drinkers, and introducing a slew of new beer brands to increase distribution efficiency.

The Right Consumer Insight

Upheaval at Miller began immediately after Philip Morris acquired it. Most of senior management was fired, and High Life was repositioned as a blue collar beer instead of the Champagne of Beers, to focus on its high-volume buyers. Their ad agency fashioned a brilliant campaign that the new management team was smart enough to sign off on.

Soon America was announcing the end of the working day with, "It's Miller time!" The phrase became ingrained in the American vocabulary—one of the hallmarks of a great buzz campaign. That buzz laid the groundwork for building the future acceptance of Lite beer from Miller.

But High Life was only half the battle. More beer brands had to be launched to drive distribution efficiencies and sales volume. Miller quickly created Miller Ale, Miller Malt Liquor, and a popular-priced beer, Milwaukee Extra.

These new brands were launched with substantial marketing budgets in multiple test markets—enough that 65 percent of their target audience would see the TV commercials at least three times a week.

Despite the backing of substantial marketing budgets, all three eventually failed to meet expectations and wasted substantial ad dollars. Lite would be different despite the cemetery of prior failures in the low-calorie category.

Philip Morris continued acquiring more beer companies for distribution efficiency. Miller's brewmaster Clem Myne took an interest in a brand from one of these companies—Lite, from Meister Brau. He improved the Lite beer recipe for taste. Remarkably, in taste tests, even drivers of beer trucks couldn't tell the difference between a regular Coors and the new Lite beer recipe.

After the brewmaster created this new recipe for Lite, ad agency McCann-Erickson was charged with discovering if Lite could become a successful national seller. They first visited Newark, New Jersey, interviewing seventy-five people who were drinking Gablinger's light beer. They discovered something that might not sound surprising today, but was a lightning bolt at the time: Heavy beer drinkers had no interest in low calories. They weren't drinking Gablinger's because of lower calorie count; they were drinking it because it didn't fill them up. A guy sitting at the bar who could down two or three regular beers could down four or five by choosing Gablinger's. And that meant hanging out longer at the bar without getting a case of beer bloat.

The Miller folks now had a hint of what could make light beer advertising succeed: Promise that it would be less filling but still good tasting. An elegant concept test was devised, measuring the appeal of three different ad messages. But they were under pressure, and test marketing would take nine to twelve months—too long. Yet without a thick scientific market research report, they had little to justify the kind of substantial ad budget that would match the budgets being lavished on Miller Malt, Miller Ale, and the other new products. The scant, informal research of seventy-five bar hounds in Newark wasn't going to do it. They needed time or they needed a miracle.

Enter a small miracle. George Weissman, president of Philip Morris, returned from a dinner with Meister Brau distributors and called a top executive of Miller Brewing. "Find out what's going on in Anderson, Indiana," he barked. "A Meister Brau distributor says he's selling Schlitz Light—and it's the *third* best selling beer in the market."

This was the trip that would spawn Lite's success. The McCann-Erickson ad agency immediately dispatched two men—Steve Norcino and Steve Tart—to Anderson, Indiana. Not Hollywood. Not Vegas. Unglamorous Anderson, Indiana. The two ad execs spent days in bars buying rounds of beers for people drinking Schlitz Light, and chatting them up to find out their reasons for drinking it . . . reasons strong enough to explain why it was the number-three beer in the market.

Again and again they heard the same refrain: "It doesn't fill me up." Again and again, they heard, "I can stay longer at the bar." It was the same story as Gablinger's, but here those reasons were strong enough to make Schlitz Light the third best-selling beer in the market. With that persuasive performance, coupled with knowing that the key to the Miller Lite advertising would be "less filling," McCann-Erickson got the nod to bypass concept testing and enter four test markets with heavy ad budgets. Now all they had to do was create advertising great enough to sell the beer, and guarantee the agency another big-ticket national campaign.

The Right Word-of-Mouth Environment

It turned out that Schlitz Light wasn't popular in Anderson because it was heavily advertised; it *wasn't* heavily advertised. The
reason was quite different: The brew had become the number-
three beer in town because it was born in the right word-of-mouth
environment—a bar. Restaurants and bars in Anderson accounted
for 75 percent of beer consumption in the town; in the rest of the
United States, it was the opposite. Nationwide, restaurants and
bars accounted for only 25 percent.

A bar by its nature is a social environment. When you order a
light beer in a bar, other people hear you ordering it. People ask. It
can start a whole conversation. And people sitting in a bar often
drink together for a few hours. There is a lot of time for talking
about a variety of things. When you go into a liquor store or supermarket to buy a six-pack, on the other hand, you're unlikely to
strike up a friendly conversation with other purchasers. At a store,
you come in, you buy, you leave.

Essentially, light beer was born in a social environment of
heavy beer drinkers, an environment that lent itself to word of
mouth—which, again, is the key ingredient of buzz.

The Right Ad Buzz

The first several attempts to create a Lite beer ad campaign fell on
their faces. Then the agency hit on a different concept, one that im-
itated the word-of-mouth environment of a local bar. The setting of
the ad was a look-alike for bars in Anderson, Indiana.

The ad showed recognizable masculine guys and ex-athletes in
a bar drinking Lite. The pictures of these well-known, macho guys
drinking Lite defused the "sissy beer" perception. At first, no one
jumped up and exclaimed, "That's it, that's the ad campaign!" But

time was running out and they needed an ad. This would have to be it—just as a stopgap until something else more solid and effective could be developed.

The slogan for the initial campaign became, "Everything you always wanted in a beer and less." Clever enough, given what they had to work with, but still a stopgap.

One of the first commercials featured Mickey Spillane, then famous as the author of a series of hard-boiled novels featuring tough-guy private eye Mike Hammer. The ad started off with a familiar opening line that set a tongue-in-cheek tone: "It was a dark and stormy night." Then Spillane talked about Lite beer as he sat at the bar. He concluded, "After all, what more could a man want on a long, lonely night?" Just as Spillane spoke this line, you saw his eyes divert to Lee Meredith, a popular actress of the day with a well-endowed chest. The answer to what men want on a long, lonely night—a Lite beer, of course!

As this Lite beer commercial aired in bars across test markets, executives from the Miller team witnessed something unusual. When the Lite commercial came on, the bar hushed. Everyone watched, and after it ended, everyone broke into conversation about the commercial.

The ad skated on the edge of what was allowable on family television without quite crossing the line. It pushed the hilarious button by offering a comedy of errors—those familiar athletes trying to act, doing it badly, and laughing at themselves—and the viewers laughing along with them. It got strangers talking to each other. It got people telling their coworkers about the funny ad with its suggestive, risky, double entendre.

Celebrity Buzz: Reality TV Before It Was Hip

Almost all of the Lite commercials from then on featured former celebrities and athletes who were just regular guys drinking beer in a bar—guys much like the very people watching the commercials. And the Lite commercials showed the foibles and idiosyncrasies of these celebrity athletes. You saw John Madden, the Super Bowl winning coach, but you saw him as the slightly wacky guy. You saw the hard-nosed Dick Butkus (once called the meanest, nastiest, fiercest linebacker ever to put on a helmet), but you saw him as the funny guy trying to convince everyone he's really quite sensitive.

Miller's approach overcame consumer resistance to ads by using celebrities in a novel way. Not "Look at me, I'm famous and I use the product, so you should too," but by positioning the celebrities in a real-people, warts-and-all view. The commercials appealed much in the way MTV's *The Newlyweds* did, by offering a view into the foibles of the famous. It's rare to see celebrity flaws revealed so openly. They fight with each other, they bark at their spouses or lovers, and, as the old line says it, they put on their pants one leg at a time—just like us. The Lite commercials proved unusual and intriguing because we rarely get a window into the *real* life of celebrities. It was reality TV before the term was invented—and it had the look of being honest.

Just as Jessica Simpson's quirks got people talking, Lite's beer commercials also got people talking—especially beer drinkers.

One commercial in particular generated tremendous buzz. Boston Celtics coach Tommy Heinsohn, famous for arguing with referees, was cast in the commercial along with referee Mendy Rudolph. Just as these two fought tooth and nail in real life on the basketball court, they fought tooth and nail at the bar in the commercial. Heinsohn argued nose to nose with the referee that Lite beer was less filling. The referee yelled back that it tastes great. "Tastes great/less filling"—the concept caught on with the public and was headed to become one of those phrases that everyone knows.

In stadiums, arenas, graduation ceremonies, and other events, a group in the crowd would spontaneously cheer "tastes great" and others would cheer "less filling." America not only talked about the commercial, they were shouting it!

In the first ten years of the campaign, eighty-one commercials were made with seventy-four different personalities. On average, a new Lite commercial came out every six weeks, and there was a new athlete or celebrity in almost every one. The campaign rarely got stale because people knew another commercial was coming soon. People looked forward to seeing them.

The commercials created so much buzz that careers took off after appearing in a Lite ad. John Madden became a network announcer after his commercials. Dick Butkus and Bubba Smith were signed to their own TV detective show. Rodney Dangerfield's Lite commercials resurrected his ailing career.

The Right Results

From the very beginning, in the four test markets, Lite took off like no other in Miller's stable of brands. It found the right ad buzz, the right positioning, and re-created itself in the right word-of-mouth buzz environment, the conversational environment of a bar.

In the Providence test market, Cliff Wilmot from Miller and Steve Tart from McCann-Erickson visited to see how the test was going. They found the local Miller distributor holding the phone arm's length away from his ear. It turned out he was talking to his number one customer in Providence, representing 20 percent of the distributor's entire sales. He stopped in mid-sentence.

"Hold on. The guys from Miller just walked in the door—you can talk to them yourself."

The Miller executive pointed to the ad exec to take the phone.

"What the hell kind of test market are you boys running" the guy on the other end of the phone shouted.

Steve responded, "I'm not sure I follow you."

"I've got no Lite beer on my warehouse floor, I've got no Lite beer on the shelf, and your distributor ain't got no Lite beer to deliver. When the hell is the beer coming?"

It was a blessing. Lite beer had sold out. The shelves in Providence were empty. The commercials had been tremendously effective.

Every other test market was the same. The ads—the buzz—worked.

Recap

The three other Miller products—Miller Malt, Miller Ale, and Milwaukee's Extra—all failed. They might have had the advantage of huge advertising budgets, but Lite was built on the right consumer insight and in the right word-of-mouth environment.

Finding the right consumer insight is your foundation for success. Positioning Lite as low-calorie beer would have turned off heavy beer drinkers. The Lite team had the knowledge and desire to ferret out the truth firsthand. They journeyed to very unsexy places like Newark, New Jersey, and Anderson, Indiana, in order to drink and talk with hundreds of people not usually sought out by the ad agencies or corporate America. They heard nuggets of truth (doesn't make you belch . . . can stay at the bar longer so you don't have to go home . . . doesn't fill you up). These early adopters could have cared less about their waistlines—they lifted more steel and moved more pallets than most of us. "Low-cal" wouldn't connect. But "less filling"—now there's something that had value.

Now let's look at Anderson, Indiana. Light beer was *not* heavily advertised in the market. Essentially, blue collar workers created their own positioning for light beer as less filling. And the product grew. Not by advertising, but because it found itself in a market where 75 percent of beer was consumed in bars and restaurants—the polar opposite of the U.S. market.

Why does it matter? Because the early growth of a brand is critically dependent on word of mouth. And if you plant your marketing seeds in an environment that fosters word of mouth (in this case, the bar environment), you're ahead of the game. If you want people to talk about your brand, get as close as possible to a demographic that talks a lot or in an environment that talks a lot.

Ultimately, Lite's journey to the second best-selling beer in America ten years later was attributed to a great tasting product, and team work: distributors building bigger warehouses and buying more trucks; Miller building more breweries and upgrading its sales systems; and so on.

But it doesn't happen without demand. And creating demand is about creating buzz.

CHAPTER FIVE

Starting Up from Scratch—
Green for Greenfield

It's one thing when a well-established company like Miller, with backing from Philip Morris, decides that one of its products deserves the buzz treatment.

But what about the small start-up company? What about the individual entrepreneur, and the professionals with a solo or small-group practice—the doctors, lawyers, plumbers, graphic artists, Web designers, and the rest? Buzz isn't for them, right?

Wrong. Pushing buttons and getting people talking is no different for the big or the small. The common denominator is getting people to talk about you, and the media to write about you. People talk one-on-one; the same principle applies regardless of size or scale.

This is a little-known story about a chiropractor who started with nothing and created a multimillion dollar business.

Jeff Greenfield grew up in a small Florida suburb. He took a liking to magic and began performing his first magic tricks at age five. By age ten, he was regularly performing at parties and events, and making more money than his mother, a registered nurse.

His specialty was close-up magic. When Uri Geller became famous for his spoon-bending trick in the 1970s, Jeff Greenfield began performing the same trick, though still a teen, and was written up in the preeminent trade publication *Magical Arts Journal.* But Jeff didn't create a multimillion-dollar business in the business of magic. He studied to become a chiropractor at a college in Los Angeles—paying his tuition and expenses as the youngest magician at an exclusive club nestled in the Hollywood Hills, the Magic Castle.

Great magicians are often great marketers. And why is that? One guess could be that magicians have well-developed skills in sleight of hand, manipulation, and misdirection—just like a lot of today's marketing. Good guess, but that's not the reason. Great magicians have two keen abilities: They understand consumer behavior—how to influence people to look in one direction, and how to communicate with people one-on-one in setting up a trick and explaining what's about to happen.

Understanding consumer behavior and communicating extremely well one-on-one are two valuable skills in business. Most marketing gets discombobulated right here, because most marketers think in terms of their messages going out to thousands. That's the stage they're given: a mass-market stage.

The traditional marketing model sends each message out to people via a one-way vehicle (even when sending one message to those watching VH1 and another one to those watching *Comedy Central*). The marketing industry has grown up taking one-way communication for granted since the 1940s.

Magicians, however, start with a two-way communication model. If people don't gasp in wonder at their trick, it's like a stand-up comedian not getting a laugh. Magicians live for interaction and two-way communication, and have to be able to understand consumer expectations, exceed them, and communicate well to get the applause. And when the audience members reward a magician with that applause, what happens? They come back from their evening at the Magic Castle, or the show in Las Vegas . . . and tell all their friends about the most amazing magician they saw.

Starting Out

On graduating from chiropractic college, Jeff Greenfield moved from Los Angeles to the suburban Boston hometown of his newly-wed wife. He had no experience setting up his own practice. He had no clients. He had no office.

Like most entrepreneurs, Jeff set up business in his house, and Jeff Greenfield Family Chiropractic was born with a shingle and a phone. The customers would have to come. That's always the hard part.

In general, dentists, chiropractors, and doctors of all kinds are fairly successful. So naturally, one would look at the existing marketing model for the industry and simply duplicate it. Convention, right? Makes sense, right? It's working for everybody else, why do anything different—right?

If you want average results, this is your ticket. But Jeff never followed convention. Most chiropractors in the Boston area had two ways of building their business: yellow pages, and the "crooked spine" pens with the doctor's name and telephone number. The problem with this method, however, is that every chiropractor in Boston does virtually the same thing. Pens are cute. They can be ordered easily, and a yellow pages ad can be placed in ten minutes.

What's easy is often what's done the most. What's done the most gets cluttered. What's cluttered doesn't grab attention. And if you can't grab attention, you can't grow your business.

Because of Jeff's background in magic, he knew that once he got attention, he could deliver an experience that would exceed people's expectations, just as when he was mystifying an audience.

So rather than follow the crowd, he took the path less traveled.

At first he attracted the patients no one wanted. All the competing chiropractors turned away people without health insurance, people able to afford only a fraction of what an insured patient's coverage would pay. His philosophy was treatment first. He never turned away anyone who needed treatment. From some patients, he got paid nothing, and from others, he got paid whatever the patient could afford.

One woman came to his practice who was homeless. She lived in her car, had no money, but was in extreme pain. Though Jeff turned no one away, he did charge in the form of word of mouth. That's how he built his business with nonpaying patients: He got them to pay with something they could afford.

First, most of his empty-pocket patients were in severely bad shape. A typical chiropractor might view this as a problem, but it was Dr. Jeff's dream. He wanted the patients no one else could cure, because when he succeeded with them, he would be viewed as the miracle worker. Patients would tell their friends, bosses, relatives, coworkers—anyone who knew them well enough to notice the dramatic difference. The patient would delightedly spread the glowing word about the amazing doctor, Jeff Greenfield. That's buzz at work.

He Didn't Care Whether a Patient Who Came Through the Door Was a Millionaire Living in a Mansion on a Hilltop or a Homeless Person Living in His Car

Besides the word-of-mouth promise, he had one other demand, an unconventional treatment schedule that went against all norms. The insurance industry essentially created a weekly schedule for patients. Every Tuesday or Thursday or whatever, you'd go in to see Dr. X. Why? Because that's what the insurance companies were willing to pay for.

Dr. Jeff, however, didn't give a hoot about the industry, he cared about the patient. Treating patients once a week was the common practice. But Jeff wanted to cure people much faster. He prescribed a schedule based on the patient, and getting that patient healed as quickly as possible—which is of course what every patient wants.

It wasn't unusual for Dr. Jeff to see the same patient six days a week for two or three months. Constant, consistent, intense care to cure the trauma of an accident or years of pent-up, chronic pain.

What happened? Exactly what Dr. Jeff expected: Patients got well fast. Amazingly well, and amazingly fast. It was not what his patients expected—to them, it was nothing short of a miracle. For the first time in years, they could walk without pain in every step.

The Two Demands

The unconventional treatment schedule that the patient had to agree to was the first piece in creating buzz: Give 'em something to talk (or rave) about; (remember this from our First Secret: Push the Six Buttons of Buzz).

So while Dr. Jeff would accept anyone, the person had to agree to these two conditions. He would look the person straight in the eye and tell them he would make them feel the best they had ever felt physically and mentally in their entire life. But only if they would commit to his two conditions. "Stick to the schedule. You can't get better if you don't show up." And, he would heal them, but only if they told every single friend, family member, and coworker about him and what benefit they were getting. And not just tell people, "Hey, I'm seeing this great chiropractor, check him out." No, Dr. Jeff wanted them to gush with zeal about "the man that's changing my entire life." To everyone. To anyone. This was the word-of-mouth promise.

And Dr. Jeff gave them a tool for this promise. Every week, he gave his patients four business cards—very nontraditional cards. On one side it read, "This entitles you to a free exam at Greenfield Family Chiropractic." But on the other side, the card had an inspirational saying.

Dr. Jeff preprinted a six-month supply of these cards with hundreds of different thoughtful messages.

One of the secrets of great marketing is not only to get people talking but to make your marketing so valuable that people collect your marketing pieces and admire them; a strategy brilliantly used by Absolut vodka, whose print ads have been considered collectibles for many years. Dropping by his suburban Boston bank once, Dr. Jeff noticed the teller had push-pinned one of the inspirational cards to the wall. You know buzz is working when it appears unexpectedly . . . and when your customers are marketing for you.

Why Targeting Doesn't Always Work

Some may say that indigents aren't the way to grow a business. But every so often, Jeff Greenfield's word of mouth would spread to somebody who had fantastic insurance; first one, then another, then a few more. Dr. Jeff got buzz. His tiny practice that had begun with down and out folks began to explode. Revenues shot up.

Tried and true marketers might caution that it would have been better to target insured patients at first. Let's ask why the conventional marketing establishment is so focused on targeting. I have the answer, and it has to do with philosophy.

The reason why targeting seems so important to the traditional marketing establishment grows from the idea of *marketing efficiency*—a principle that says "Only spend money sending messages to people in your customer demographic." Yes, you definitely want to be in the ballpark of the demographics. But for the most part, the principle turns out to be utter poppycock. Marketing efficiency sounds fancy and important. It communicates largess and fiduciary responsibility with marketing dollars. Hell, it sounds like something I would advise.

But marketing efficiency and targeting become important only if you've got nothing buzzworthy. In other words, if your message is so commonplace that no one will tell two friends, and so on, and so on, then you're in big trouble, and you better target till the cows come home.

But indigents who tell four people every week for two or three months with unequivocal zeal come in contact with people from many walks of life. They aren't the richest, but they may have family members who work for lawyers or businesspeople or shop owners. Some of them might even drink coffee next to a millionaire at Dunkin' Donuts.

Word of mouth, if it's good (I'll give the yardsticks for measuring *good* in a later chapter), crosses class barriers, gender barriers, income barriers, and education barriers. The buzzmarketing model is based on a philosophy that targeting isn't fully necessary, because buzz will spread further and wider. When it comes to word of mouth, the key to success is reach, not frequency. If the story is good enough, it only takes one time to have an impact, while traditional advertising requires multiple attempts to have a prayer of impact.

Dr. Jeff's practice explodes . . . and what happens next becomes both an asset and a problem. He's been seeing patients in his house, so, unlike 99 percent of chiropractors in the Boston suburbs, he has no patient waiting room and no patient examination rooms. He also doesn't have the financial resources for a "real" doctor's office.

But the problem with patient rooms and waiting rooms in nearly every doctor's office is just that. There's a hell of a lot of waiting . . . and a hell of a lot of patience required by the patient. You wait thirty or forty-five minutes after arriving on time.

So Dr. Jeff set up a system in his home office where the treatment tables were sitting right next to each other. No walls. The tables were three feet apart, lined up like a factory. Patients lay ready for Dr. Jeff, but waited no more than five minutes. Dr. Jeff also knew many of his patients worked during the day, so he kept office hours as late as 9 P.M.

While the typical chiropractic office was seeing thirty patients a day per chiropractor, Dr. Jeff was seeing 125 to 150 patients a day. And when you see 125 to 150 patients a day, six days a week, fifty-two weeks a year, all of whom are spreading the word of mouth the way Dr. Jeff's patients were . . . your business grows exponentially.

Customers of other chiropractors in his area began to discover Dr. Jeff, and began defecting to his practice. Buzz creates a stir by breaking convention and audaciously threatening the status quo.

And the keepers of the status quo did indeed feel threatened. Local chiropractors didn't like losing patients and revenue to Greenfield Family Chiropractic. In fact, they hated it. Some hated it so much that Dr. Jeff began receiving death threats, and security guards were hired to watch his house/office twenty-four hours a day.

Now it was time to get a "real" doctors office. The formula didn't change. Unconventional scheduling, fast visits, word of mouth buzz. But Dr. Jeff got a much larger office than required . . . intending to accommodate future growth.

Here comes phase two of any entrepreneurial business. If you're lucky enough to make it past the birth of your business, you might feel that almost inevitable temptation to take on more fixed costs: more staff, more locations, larger or fancier space with higher rent, etc.

That story was captured on television in 2003 with NBC's *The Restaurant.* Successful entrepreneur wants to get bigger, but sometimes it just doesn't work out. You increase overhead, and you need to be *even more* successful. Sometimes growth calls for a new plan. But most who implement a new plan decide that what they need is to be like their larger, more established competitors. They start following convention and becoming more cautious.

Dr. Jeff didn't go down that path. Instead, he implemented a new plan to cover more overhead. But no, it wouldn't launch a plan that looked like the big guys. Jeff's started like this: He was still a magician at heart and felt at home performing for people. He remembered the days when he was the youngest performer at the Magic Castle and one of the best of young magicians. If you excel at something, leverage it. That's exactly what he did.

He decided to perform for people, just as he had done in his Los Angeles days. But this time, he would perform a different kind of magic. He began booking people for a free dinner at a local restaurant in exchange for a chance to tell them about his practice. Why dinner? He was used to this environment. But most important, Dr. Jeff knew something about attention. He knew that in order to get people's attention for an involved decision, he had to get their attention while they were relaxed, receptive, and rewarded. And he had to give them something before asking for something.

Free dinner at an upscale restaurant along with a drink of their choice got people relaxed, receptive, and rewarded. With a subject of interest, he grabbed 100 percent of their attention. No distractions, no competing media. Undivided attention.

And every week, Dr. Jeff would have forty people on Monday night and another forty on Tuesday night, listening to him talk about stress, sources of mental and physical pain, chronic fatigue, and solutions that included his chiropractic service, holistic health, and physiological knowledge.

Every Monday and Tuesday night, Dr. Jeff would perform. As a magician, he understood people, he understood their assumptions. He accessed these assumptions, erased many myths associated with these assumptions, and replaced certain fictions with facts. He called this his Access, Erase, Replace approach. He would speak and then offer a free tour of his new facility. Ninety-five percent of people who showed up scheduled a tour, and 70 percent of those who toured became patients.

And 70 percent of those patients recruited family, friends, neighbors, or coworkers as new patients through word of mouth. Over and over again, Dr. Jeff invited eighty prospects to dinner and ended up with ninety-three total customers. Almost unheard of in the world of marketing.

Here's the math:

950 leads = 80 prospects invited
80 prospects x 95 percent scheduling free tour = 76
76 leads take free tour x 70 percent conversion to customer = 53

53 customers, 70 percent recruit average of one friend = 40
53 + 40 = 93 total customers
950 leads/93 total customers = 10 percent response rate

A 10 percent response rate. How did he get those people to show up in the first place? Here's how.

Small businesses by nature are local. Dr. Jeff personally selected local businesses and lunch restaurants in his area. He created a form and provided a Lucite collection box at each place. What was advertised was "A free dinner & speech on stress, sources of mental and physical pain, chronic fatigue." The headline was a grabber: "What we have to say about your health may change your life." A killer headline (see more on the value of a headline in chapter 14) and a handy response mechanism got leads flowing.

The catch is . . . unconventional thinking and hard work. Yes, it sucks to ask four hundred local businesses to place a Lucite box by their cash register, and have only one hundred agree. And, yes, it's not easy to coordinate weekly pick-up and processing of the forms. It's also not easy to make sure your telemarketers get their act together to contact the selected people, call them up, fill forty seats a night twice a week, and coordinate dinners for all those people, fifty weeks a year. It's nowhere as easy as ordering crooked spine pens, or yellow pages ads.

Ask most marketing agencies today for an evaluation of this plan (without telling them the amazing results) and most would tell you they would prefer to do something else, something with more proven results. But getting buzz is about breaking through the clutter, following the path less traveled, getting attention, and getting people to talk about your business. No one ever said it would be easy. If it's easy, it probably *won't* get attention. If it's easy, it'll probably get conventional results.

That's not what Dr. Jeff did, and his results were amazing. He succeeded in phase two of the entrepreneur's journey: taking on more overhead and taking the business to the next level. Getting past phase one is often difficult enough, but succeeding in phase two is even more difficult.

The End of the Story

The story of Greenfield Family Chiropractic is the story of how a multimillion-dollar business was built with a focus on getting consumers' attention one person at a time—not millions of ad exposures at a time. Dr. Jeff found a clever way to get people talking about him and his business fast—amazingly fast. Ultimately, customers come in one person at a time, and your approach needs to speak to people not in terms of demographic profiles but as individuals.

Dr. Jeff built Greenfield Family Chiropractic into a powerful enterprise paying the salaries of seventy-five employees and changing people's lives by the score. So what happened next?

Dr. Jeff created an amazing business by getting buzz and delivering a standout product. But he discovered that along the way he had turned into a businessman who had no time to spend with patients, no time for much of anything but managing a corporate machine.

Well he had achieved success, but the future depends on how one defines success. For me, I thought rising to a position where I had responsibility for a $40 million annual marketing budget was the dream job I had been waiting for all my life. But once I got there, I found myself in a creatively constrained, no-risk, vanilla environment. I left for the world of start-ups.

And one day Dr. Jeff decided that success wasn't defined by an income statement and that the work wasn't bringing him satisfaction any more. So he sold the business to the chiropractors in his company.

But buzzmarketers never seem to stop. Without the credentials of a Harvard M.B.A. or proving himself in the executive suite of a

Ford or an Apple Computer, Dr. Jeff remains one of the smartest marketers I have ever met.

For the past ten years he's been residing on the coast of New England, becoming a secret marketing resource to the likes of those who've developed entertainment blockbusters like the Backstreet Boys and *NSYNC, and has been the secret weapon to many major product launches. His latest protégé is his tween pop-rapper Dahv, a singer now touring the country, cutting her first CD, and opening for top ten bands.

With magic from one of the best marketers in the country, expect to see Dahv hit the charts soon!

CHAPTER SIX

American Idol

We learn invaluable lessons about buzzmarketing by probing into the buzz successes of big brands and small start-ups. There are fascinating lessons, as well, in the stories of winner entertainment brands like American Idol. The intriguing twist about *American Idol* is that the show almost didn't make it to network TV.

Simon Fuller, Simon Cowell, and *American Idol's* production company, Fremantle Media, were enjoying success in the UK, South Africa, and Poland with a version called *Pop Idol,* but Hollywood executives showed little interest in signing the *Idol* show for American television.

One major network didn't even want to hear the pitch because it thought this talent search show could never get viewership. (That network will remain unnamed).

The pitch process Fremantle Media went through trying to sell the show was as disheartening as the experience that many of its contestants go through *on* the show today.

The WB channel had launched a somewhat similar program called *Pop Stars* that aired for just one season. At its peak, it pulled in a respectable three million plus viewers before ending in 2002.

Fairly decent, but no blockbuster hit. Based on that lackluster performance, executives throughout the industry were gun-shy. They also thought the music industry was too fragmented, with such widely diverse tastes—Justin Timberlake to Radiohead, Outkast to Norah Jones—that there wasn't enough of a common denominator to capture the attention of a large American audience.

But someone in Hollywood did take notice. Not former Fox head Sandy Grushow, a Hollywood vet with years of experience. And not a string of one after another Hollywood veterans, including those who passed on the pitch entirely. It took a younger maverick with surfer/rock-star looks and a warm smile: Mike Darnell, head dude of reality programming at Fox. Darnell's a dead ringer for the guys working at the Starbucks down the street from everywhere, but he's the one who made the bucks for Fox. Grande.

When Darnell is asked about what he looks for in selecting reality programming, he says all he wants is a show that will "get noticed and talked about. The thing that gets my excitement up . . . is when the buzz gets going."

Get buzz, get ratings.

Darnell makes it sound simple, but recognizing the buzz from the baloney isn't easy. He understands it, and perhaps without him and Rupert Murdoch, *Idol* might never have arrived on American shores.

But the proof is in the numbers. The graph depicts the Tuesday night ratings of the first three seasons. In its very first season, the show pulled an average of twelve million viewers. Amazing for a debut show to jump into the Nielsen Top 20 list—even *Seinfeld* didn't do that its first year. In its most recent season, *Idol* was averaging more than twenty-five million viewers a week, making it a staple in Nielsen's Top Five list. American as apple pie.

Each year more than fifty new TV shows are introduced to the American public. WB's *Pop Stars* looked somewhat similar to *Idol,* and this was the model fresh in the mind of Hollywood decision mak-

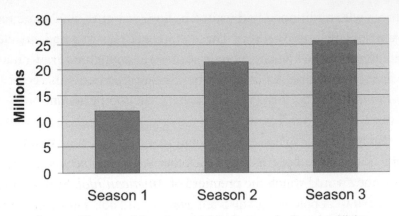

Average Viewers of *American Idol* by Season for Tuesday Nights
(Source: Fox/Nielsen)

ers. But *Idol* took off and got buzz while *Pop Stars* never really did. *Idol* succeeded at creating a formula of buzz that *Pop Stars* didn't.

The show itself cultivated a built-in audience before it even aired—not by using mass-market ads, but by connecting one-on-one with thousands of people auditioning, and also by going on the air in the summer when fewer new shows are launched so that they had less competition for viewers.

The show gave people something to talk about every week by pushing tried and true buttons for stimulating conversation—controversy with Simon Cowell (you remember the First Secret of Buzzmarketing, right? Push those buttons!). But most important, it delivered an honest, entertaining product.

With any business, franchise, or brand, half the battle is getting the consumer's attention. Consciously or not, *American Idol*'s production company, Fremantle Media, captured people's attention far ahead of the show ever airing. They gathered a built-in audience of ten thousand fans across six cities, people who had turned up for the auditions and now were anxious to watch the show.

Although ten thousand people doesn't sound like a wide reach in the world of marketing and advertising, these ten thousand people who auditioned had waited in line for hours, and some had even slept in line for days. These were people who had no idea whether the show would even be successful enough to draw an audience beyond the contestants' friends and families. But they had been willing to give hours and days of their time in the hope of making their dreams come true.

Only thirty of those ten thousand made it onto the air, and despite how dejected or frustrated the other 9,970 people were, sure as nuts, they would watch the premiere of *American Idol.* Sure as nuts, those 9,970 people would also tell every friend and family member: "I was *this close* to making it onto *American Idol.*" This is what I call face-to-face attention. It's in-person, and it's buzz in its purest form.

Not only did Freemantle capture the in-person attention of all those hopefuls, it gave them the buzz currency to tell all their friends about their brush with fame. When that show first aired, it had a ready-made audience, amplified by the word of mouth from ten thousand people who had told all their friends—and all of them just salivating to see the show.

Professor Robert Thompson captured this in his statement that "[*American Idol*] is to *Star Search* what modern quantum physics is to Newtonian gravitational equations. It's big, so much more sophisticated and so much more conscious of how you gather an audience."

Skeptical that the free promotion of those ten thousand could have made that much difference?

Consider this. A. J. Gil was a seventeen-year-old living in Seattle— one of thousands who auditioned. Radio stations camped outside the auditions, looking to fill air time with a quirky talent search story. A. J. became the only one from the Seattle area to make it to Hollywood, and got local press as a result. But well before he journeyed to Hollywood, A. J. was already so famous because of the local publicity that he was signing more than two hundred autographs a day. Long-forgotten elementary school buddies contacted him. Everywhere he went, he would get stopped—all before he even stepped on a plane.

All this when he hadn't yet appeared on television? "No way," you say.

Yes way. It's the power of attention—face-to-face attention. Ask Jay Leno. Leno stops to shake just about every hand and sign every autograph. Why? Because he knows the power of face-to-face attention. He subscribes to a mantra of Lyndon Johnson's: "One handshake is worth 250 votes." In order to maintain his 44 percent ratings lead over the next closest late night competitor, Leno operates on a marketing diet of hard work and as much face-to-face as he can squeeze in, doing more than a hundred live appearances a year outside of *The Tonight Show*. If you ever shake Jay's hand, you'll probably tell all your friends and family, and you can imagine them telling their friends and family, adding up to Lyndon Johnson's 250 people quite quickly.

Face-to-face attention may start small, but it captures attention like no other means on earth.

Attention: The Law of Statistics

"The fall line-up"—you've heard the term: Most debut TV shows launch in fall. Why? In summer, ratings drop as we spend more time outside, spend more time traveling and vacationing. Fall comes, the weather grows cooler, it gets dark earlier, and we watch more TV. Ratings begin to build in fall. So the conventional wisdom says, "Launch a new show in the fall." Perhaps one part logic, one part tradition. But launching a show during the summer when TV ratings drop off entirely? Not a new phenomenon, but not exactly the norm.

The key driver to capturing attention is what you compete against. Imagine launching a new TV show in fall, competing with fifteen other new shows. Statistically, you've got a one in fifteen chance of making it. By the very nature of competing with fewer competitors and less clutter you have a better chance of capturing a consumer's attention.

Some in the media were perplexed at the timing of *American Idol*'s summer launch. But look at the pluses: First, the show would compete against fewer new offerings. Second, it would reach a key demographic group with time on their hands: the twenty-one-and-unders, a highly viral bunch who are out of school and have plenty of extra time to watch TV and consume all forms of entertainment.

Attention Basics 101: To get attention, you need fewer competitors vying for it.

Attention: Controversy

In America, most of us were raised to be polite. How often did our parents tell us, "If you can't say something nice, don't say anything at all." Except for political commentators, sports writers, and (sometimes) movie critics, most of us sugarcoat the truth.

Enter Simon Cowell, the cocreator of *Idol*. When the cameras are rolling, it's all business. He's blunt, sometimes rude, and doesn't sugarcoat anything. When it comes to judging on camera, he says things even when he knows they will hurt the contestant to hear.

Yet sources at Fremantle Media and former *American Idol* finalists refer to Simon as one of the smartest businessmen and insist he's playing a role. Unlike what you might expect from his on-screen personality, he's extremely courteous off-camera to lowly interns and bigwigs alike. Always saying "please" and "thank you."

On the air, he's a man who knows that controversy generates more buzz and thus higher ratings. The character that Simon plays—the villain—pushes people's buttons, makes people gasp, and makes people seethe. Without a doubt, it creates controversy. Viewers love it and can't get enough of dramatic cutting remarks like these:

"My advice would be if you want to pursue a career in the music business—don't."

"Did you really believe you could become the American Idol? Well, then, you're deaf."

"Boy band, yes. American Idol, no."

"One of them doesn't look good, and the other one looks amazing. The uglier one has a better voice than the good-looking one . . ."

"All of this pretend hugging, it's [bleep]. These people should hate each other's guts. Why should they want another contestant to do well?"

"Randy's okay. Paula's a pain in the ass. She's just one of those irritating people."

Simon creates controversy with outrageous and taboo remarks. He's a shock to the American culture, and we salivate for his next zinger each week—compelled to talk about it and read about it the next day. He continually creates controversy for our entertainment pleasure. He's got our goat, he's captured our attention. And we're glued.

Sustaining Buzz—An Honest Product That Delivers

So we're stuck to our TV screens watching, listening, and waiting with baited breath to hear Simon say exactly what we're all thinking (but would be too polite to vocalize to an earnest competitor). Eventually, though, even the novelty of the tight T-shirt-wearing, insult-slinging Brit can wear off. The buzz dies down, it fades, or worse yet—it turns on you. After you've got attention, you ultimately have to deliver a great product that can create buzz on its own. If you don't deliver, you'll get the wrong kind of buzz—bad buzz—which spreads even faster. Good buzz can turn into bad buzz (we'll get to this later; it's the Sixth Secret) as fast as it takes Paula to offer up an undeserved compliment. Don't invest your efforts in capturing the most precious thing of all—attention—if you have just an average product that doesn't excite, or inspire word-of-mouth conversation.

And here's where *American Idol* can teach American business a truckload. First, the show captures our attention, pushes our buttons, and gives us something to talk about at the watercooler the next day. But it doesn't suppose that's enough to sustain us. It knows that the one thing it really has going for it—the one thing that separates it from so many of the other reality shows out there—is honesty.

Compare *Idol* to, say, *The Bachelor*. Perhaps in earlier episodes of *Bachelor* we were able to suspend disbelief—we wanted to think true love really could be found on TV. But, season after season, we see the aftermath: "*Bachelor* Relationship Over!"—splashed across the front cover of every tabloid at the checkout line. All signs point to one conclusion: *The Bachelor* is kind of a sham. Their ratings begin to slump. Even Harry Winston stops offering up engagement rings for the show.

Parse the words, and technically we may not have been lied to, but we're sick of having to read the fine print—that goes for marketing, especially because it's in our face so much of the time. We were misled by Enron, and a ton of Americans lost their savings. We were misled by Mr. Clinton's convincing assertion that he did not do a certain thing with a certain young woman.

With *American Idol,* there's no misleading, there's no fine print. What you see is what you get. Simon has no qualms "scratching" with his middle finger, though he denied it was what it looked like. Perhaps he was being more honest than we're used to in America.

And the finalists? They're pretty honest themselves—not Hollywood thin or Hollywood beautiful. They're a bit geeky, sometimes a bit chunky, and often not the most popular kids in school. To viewers, they're very much like "us folks." They're shooting for the universal success story: Hometown boy or girl makes good. Better than good—famous.

Clearly, *American Idol* isn't a show based on buzz or hype, shine or polish. It is, essentially, a show about honesty. And it even invites us, the viewer, to participate in that honesty by putting a million-dollar recording contract, not in the hands of corporate management, but in the hands of ordinary people. We watch. We call in. And we, the people, vote. In a time when so many of us feel disempowered, *American Idol* gives us one brief moment every week when we're in control.

Pushing the Button of Secrecy

At around 2:00 A.M. after every Tuesday night *Idol* performance, four people know the secret of who's won: the guardian of the telephone voting operation, Sandy King; Cecile Frot-Coutaz from Fremantle Media; the president of Fox Television; and one person from Fox's office of Standards & Practices (the networks' euphemistic name for the censors).These four keep the answers under security as tight as Fort Knox. Despite pleas to know the outcome from high level Fox executives, the list of those in the know doesn't change. Not even the phone company knows how many people voted for each of the contestants. Four people, that's it.

Secrecy begs speculation.

And speculation leads to—you guessed it—*buzz.* Maybe *Idol* has other good reasons for keeping mum on the subject, but its secrecy helps fuel a media frenzy. In fact, along with Simon's brutal critiques and the show's inherent honesty, the secrecy surrounding it keeps viewers hanging to such a point that office pools across America have their own winner's brackets (much like the NCAA

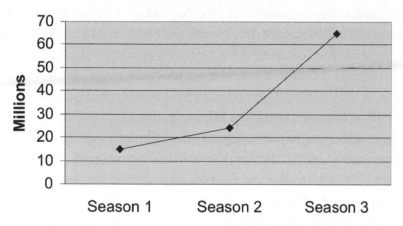

Number of Votes Cast for Final Episode of *American Idol* in First Three Seasons
(SOURCE: FOX TV)

March Madness brackets for winning teams), and *Idol* has every entertainment journalist writing furiously into the night in order to make the entertainment section deadline.

Secrets give way to speculation, outcomes give way to outcry, and buzz begets more buzz. The sixty-five million votes cast in the season three final episode say it all.

A Funny Thing Happened on the Way to the Cell Phone

Fremantle and Fox haven't been the only ones to benefit from the popularity of the show. The cell phone industry hit payday, too, when they hitched their ride to the *Idol* train. Here's how it all went down.

Imagine you're launching a new product for a major wireless company. You hire a big agency; they come up with a sharp campaign, something totally different, really off-the-wall. You spend $120 million on advertising. And nothing happens.

Ooops.

Welcome to the story of mLife, from AT&T Wireless—perhaps the greatest example of how to waste $120 million of corporate money. The name confused people so much that the company was mistaken for MetLife. On top of that, MetLife sued for trademark infringement. Nothing happens *and* you get sued. Ooops, again.

Lesson learned. AT&T Wireless tries again. This time, though, they're aiming high—by trying to talk people into using something called SMS (for short messaging service; today we call it text messaging). The technology works; companies in Europe and Asia were selling a ton of it. But in America, the effort represented nothing short of trying to change consumer behavior. And they decided that a great ad platform to introduce America to this new idea would be the ultimate advertising beauty pageant: the 2003 edition of the Super Bowl.

This idea is so genius, in fact, that both AT&T and its competitor, Sprint PCS, buy spots. Good thing they weren't actually on the field, though, because in their game, neither team won. AT&T lost another round: one more big advertising spend with little return.

Text Messaging Meets *American Idol*

It's January 2003, season two of *American Idol,* and the audience is given the opportunity, for the first time, to cast votes by text message. In one request, *American Idol* did for text messaging what the biggest and best ad agencies couldn't do.

American Idol taught America how to text. Big time. In 2003, 7.5 million text votes were sent in to the show, and 33 percent of those people had never before sent a text message in their lives. In 2004, 13.5 million text votes were cast.

In those two seasons, more than 7 million people learned how to text message because of *American Idol.* Jupiter Research Analyst

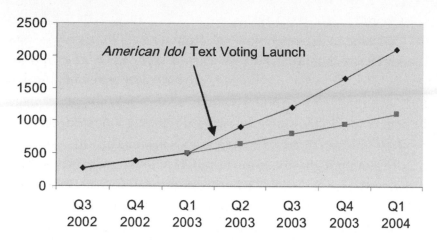

Verizon's Text Message Volume by Quarter, in Thousands of Voice; Actual Versus Projected Baseline (162 percent impact)

Avi Greengart stated that *"American Idol* probably did more to popularize SMS than anything else."

According to technology research firm InStat/MDR, overall U.S. text message volume rose from 11.9 billion messages in 2003 to a projected 30.2 billion in 2004.

Single-handedly, *American Idol* exploded the text message marketplace and taught America how to text.

Power to the People

So *Idol* has America text messaging like never before, but the question still remains: How were they able to introduce a completely unfamiliar technology to their audience and actually get them to start using it? The answer is "Empowered Interactivity."

You've likely heard of interactivity before—getting your audience, reader, or consumer involved and interacting with your product; moving them out of the role of passive observer. But empowered interactivity takes that one step further by giving the user a reason to be invested in your brand or product. You connect them to it by empowering them. In *American Idol*'s case, they allow us, their audience, to vote for who wins and who loses. And in return? We talk. We spread the gospel. We may not be up on stage singing our hearts out, but we are still very much a part of *American Idol.*

Need further proof of the impact of empowered interactivity? Just imagine if *Idol* solicited you to vote for your favorite performer of the week—but your vote had no impact, no power, no effect. In this scenario, we would see far fewer votes being cast. The subtle but important difference is: Your vote counts. Real, observable results of your voting are seen the very next day when one *Idol* wannabe is sent packing.

As part of its product, *Idol* made empowered interactivity a key driver. In fact, the voting itself (and the outcome of the voting) becomes the costar of every episode. Without voting from everyday people, the show couldn't work.

Consider this. A neighbor of mine told me a story about a local political party that approached him. Before they went into full diatribe, he simply cut to the chase and asked, "What do you want, my money or my time? I'll give you my money but not my time." Time: perhaps the most valued commodity in our modern-day economy, next to ideas, and, of course, money.

So when people devote their time to watching and voting, they're investing a valuable (and highly coveted) part of themselves. What's more, these "empowered" people become your best customers.

Let Your Customers Do the Selling for You

At Half.com, we discovered that buyers who left feedback ratings for sellers spent dramatically more money than most consumers. Very similar to the successful eBay model, Half created a mechanism for empowered interactivity, and the customers who took part, investing their time and effort, not only became our biggest brand fans who spread word of mouth but also spent significantly more money.

Though perhaps empowered interactivity may not be mainstream to the world of marketing, it isn't entirely foreign to those successful in the music industry. Pros like Johnny and Donna Wright would often take a rough cut of budding (or even already popular) music artists to DJs in key music markets like Los Angeles. They would ask the DJs for suggestions for improving a particular song; perhaps one DJ would suggest ending the song on a longer, lower note versus a high, short note. When the album was finally released, any DJ whose suggestion had been used was a good deal more likely to give that song airplay because, quite simply, they felt invested in it. Low-tech but highly effective empowered interactivity.

Radio Disney is another empowered interactivity success story. Reaching 5.2 million kids and moms each week, Radio Disney practically built its franchise on getting listeners invested and involved. In their case, fans, not DJs, determine the playlist. Here's how it works.

There are three buckets of songs; they will get played fourteen times a week, or thirty-five times a week, or seventy-seven times a week. Programming execs like Robin Jones and her team determine which songs get debuted into the fourteen-a-week category. Sometimes it's because a programming executive received a CD from a label, or sometimes it's because thousands of fans called in and asked Radio Disney to play songs they've heard on the Internet or from local groups or singers.

Once a song is in the fourteen-a-week category, its fate is determined by a tabulation of requests from fans calling the Radio Disney 800 number. Every seven days, call-in requests are tabulated and finalized. Based on the "votes," the song's position on the playlist is set—not by "the suits," but by eight-year-olds.

In the case of Fremantle Media and *American Idol,* is it really Fremantle's show, or is it perhaps the fans' show?

The key to making interactivity work is to turn it into empowered interactivity. Though the difference between the two may at first appear subtle, it's actually huge. Ask people to vote just for fun, where their vote has no real impact, and you'll find they simply won't participate to the same degree. And that translates to less word-of-mouth buzz. But create a mechanism for empowered interactivity where people have an observable impact, and it becomes their brand, their fifteen minutes of fame, their outcome. They contributed to the success of the brand, they now possess the buzz currency, and they promote it. It's an incredibly powerful and virtually free marketing tool.

Recap

The strangest thing about the *American Idol* story is that people from British-based Fremantle Media knew *Idol* would succeed, but found they had to put countless hours and months of effort into getting just one network to sign up for *American Idol.*

What Fremantle brought to America wasn't just a show, but a formula for success. Their battle for attention was waged on multiple fronts. Without Mike Darnell recognizing the buzz factor of *Idol* and taking a risk, it might not have happened at all. Without Simon's antics, the buzz might have fizzed. And without a solid, honest product at the end, people might have tuned in, only to quickly tune out. *Idol* got buzz and got big (now in more than thirty countries, from Norway to China).

Quite often we find brands or products that capture initial attention, but fail to deliver consistently. What we may never notice are the products that make money and may actually be better than their competitors, but have had difficulty cracking the code of buzz (think eCount vs. PayPal).

What makes *American Idol* a buzz blockbuster? It fails on no front. It caught our attention. It pushed our buttons and got us talking. It showed its warts, not just its polish. It delivered a great product, and created a means for empowered interactivity to take root, making us, its viewers, the costars every Wednesday night.

Copycats will come and go, but expect this brand to continue topping the ratings and capturing the media.

And how can a business person like you capture the media? It's not as you might think. That's coming up next.

CHAPTER SEVEN

The Second Secret—Capture Media

People don't buy *Time*, *Newsweek*, and *USA Today* to read the advertising. They buy publications like these to read the articles. What's the most beautiful thing about the news media? It already has consumer attention.

Historically, the media has been called the "fourth estate" to keep politicians and corporate America in check. A reporter has no incentive to make up false claims and, subsequently, carries far more weight than an advertisement. So when the media writes about a product, people tend to believe the reporting is credible.

So the media shares the two critical components of word-of-mouth marketing: attention and credibility. The media has your attention (much more so than advertising). The media has credibility.

And guess what? Because it has people's attention and is credible, the media acts as an amplifier for your product.

How much can it amplify? The late advertising guru David Ogilvy discovered that roughly six times as many people read the average news article versus the average advertisement. Ogilvy's six-times factor still holds true today—I've personally experienced a 6.2-times increase in response by using a nontraditional advertising method (which you'll read about in a later story) that was amplified by the press.

How Media Coverage Leads to Ads Getting Read

Let's understand how this works. I was advertising a product using some innovative, alternative methods, and the media picked up on it. Even without spending any more on the advertising, because the media picked it up, we saw a huge increase in the response rate to our ads.

Why do you get a huge impact on your ads as a result of editorial mentions?

When you create a buzz in the media, people want to know what all the buzz is about. When Ford launched the Mustang, it saw amazing 95 percent readership scores from its print ads. Why? Because there was a buzz about the Mustang, and people wanted to have a better understanding of the product. Mustang buzz was on people's radar, and they were curious about everything Mustang . . . even ads.

Same advertising, same cost—but much higher impact when the media amplifies your current ad dollars. Capturing the attention of the media is valuable, but marketing *plus* media buzz is priceless.

So now you're interested in capturing media attention to amplify your marketing? You wouldn't mind a six-fold increase in the effectiveness of your ad dollars? You're catching on. But what captures the media like flypaper?

The media, my friend, is the most predictable industry in America. I grew up in a family newspaper business where the name of the game was to deliver high-quality stories of interest and, ultimately, increase the number of papers sold. Each week, I witnessed my father deliberate which story and headline would make the front page of our Cape Cod newspapers and which would not.

What would get people to buy our newspaper over the competitor's newspaper? From a marketer's perspective, knowing what gets press is the key to success. It's pretty simple.

Below are the five most frequently written news stories in America. Deliver a ready-made story that's also one of the five most frequently written stories . . . and you're on the right road to capturing media attention.

The Five Most Frequently Written Stories

Similar in many ways to giving consumers something to talk about—you've got to give the media something to write about. The media's appetite for what's newsworthy is slightly different from the consumer's.

Year after year, the five most frequently written news stories are the following:

- The David-and-Goliath story
- The unusual or outrageous story
- The controversy story
- The celebrity story
- What's already hot in the media

If you can create a story with any of these story angles you're going to capture the media attention. Create a story that packs two, three, or four of these angles, and you've got a grand slam!

Maxim 1: Create a David-and-Goliath Story to Capture the Media

For thousands of years, we've been telling generation after generation the story of David and Goliath. This is a story that America itself personifies. Dating all the way back to Bunker Hill, America was the underdog that won its fight for independence against the stronger, more powerful British forces. America was the underdog. America loves the underdog. The American media loves to write about the underdog. It does so time and time again.

DAVID AND GOLIATH, EXAMPLE 1: KIWI AIRLINES

Back in the early 1990s, the airline industry was in shambles. The U.S. economy fell into recession, and airlines were laying off personnel left and right. Giants like Eastern Airlines folded entirely. But in a little house in Bayonne, New Jersey, a handful of laid-off pilots started their own airline.

One thing they needed was a name. New American, Phoenix, and Kiwi were three names on the table. Although Phoenix was a favorite, symbolizing the return of these aging pilots from the ashes, Kiwi was chosen because it was a nickname for pilots who weren't flying—just like the Kiwi bird, which doesn't fly. While some criticize the name for its connection with an exotic fruit as well as for the flightless bird, the ironic name alone would indeed capture the media, promising to lead to stories about an airline that wasn't supposed to get off the ground in one of the worst aviation economies of time, but did get off the ground anyway.

Kiwi Airlines went against the grain and stood out. When layoffs were rampant elsewhere in the industry, Kiwi was busy hiring the laid-off workers. When most airlines raised prices to bolster sagging profits, Kiwi touted the lowest rates on the East Coast. It was the epitome of contrarianism in a world of airline carnage. The Kiwi name itself symbolized it was the David to awaken Goliath.

On its very first flight, the analogous story of the Kiwi bird defying nature captured the attention of the media. The airline became the young darling of the press. When a reporter questioned the Continental Airlines CEO Bob Crandall about Kiwi, he spoke disparagingly of the start-up. Inadvertently, his remarks created a David-and-Goliath story. The media got hooked, and the story spawned a life of its own.

Weeks after Crandall's remarks, Continental Airlines slashed prices on routes only where they competed with Kiwi. They even slashed prices during the Thanksgiving blackout, a time when no airline slashed prices because Thanksgiving passenger capacity approaches 100 percent. At any cost, Continental aimed to crush Kiwi.

Kiwi didn't sit idle. It saw the opportunity to create even more of a David-and-Goliath story . . . and that it did.

Within days, Kiwi issued a press release accusing Continental of violating federal predatory pricing laws. Kiwi began legal proceedings with the U.S. Department of Transportation, though the DOT had historically taken a hands-off approach to predatory pricing. At the time, the Clinton administration had just taken office, and the DOT didn't know what position the new administration wanted it to take.

The David-and-Goliath story couldn't have been better.

At first it was Kiwi versus Continental Airlines. But now, it was Kiwi versus big government. The *Wall Street Journal,* CNBC, CNN, and all the major networks picked up the story. Kiwi Airlines was now taking off.

DAVID AND GOLIATH, EXAMPLE 2: BEN & JERRY'S

Ben & Jerry's also took off by creating a David-and-Goliath story. I had the opportunity to peek into the mind of former Ben & Jerry's CEO Chico Lager and gain insight on how this fledging company catapulted into the national spotlight, doubling its normal sales trajectory.

In the early 1980s, Ben & Jerry's was selling what was arguably the best packaged ice cream in the country, mostly through outlets in Vermont. Around that time, the company received outside funding to expand into new markets, and their first market was Boston.

One of the key factors in penetrating markets: Get large distributors to sell your product. Distributors not only have the physical trucks and infrastructure, they have the key relationships with stores. Ben & Jerry's signed up with Paul's Distributors to penetrate the Boston market.

Although Ben & Jerry's was just beginning to crack the Boston market, Häagen-Dazs didn't like what it saw. They were the number-one ice cream, with 100 percent penetration in every supermarket. An important client of any ice cream distributor, Häagen-Dazs gave Paul's an ultimatum: Stop distributing Ben & Jerry's or lose the entire Häagen-Dazs business.

Given Häagen-Dazs's huge market share, ignoring the ultimatum would have amounted to financial ruin for Paul's. A panicked call came in to Ben Cohen, cofounder and the "Ben" of Ben & Jerry's, asking him to come to Boston immediately. The distributor anxiously explained his dilemma to Cohen.

Cohen didn't flinch, but instead felt complimented that two hippies who founded Ben & Jerry's had Häagen-Dazs, part of Pillsbury's huge $4 billion conglomerate, shaking in its boots. Ben Cohen didn't envision a declining sales line at all. In fact, he saw opportunity.

What he did was create a David-and-Goliath story. Winning a court case would be very expensive: Pillsbury was two thousand times the size of Ben & Jerry's. So Chico Lager and Ben Cohen decided to wage their battle in the minds of consumers and in the media. It was a David-and-Goliath story made to order.

The marketing and media campaign began right away. Ben & Jerry's issued a press release announcing that the fight against Pillsbury's unfair practices would begin with a request for a federal restraining order. The press release also illustrated the disparity of size between the two companies, stating that Ben & Jerry's total sales were just "a little more than what Pillsbury gave its president and [its] chairman in compensation."

As the campaign battle cry, Chico Lager created the slogan "What's the doughboy afraid of?" Pulled out of semiretirement, cofounder Jerry Greenfield conducted a one-man picketing effort in front of Pillsbury's headquarters. For a week, Jerry handed out leaflets protesting that Pillsbury was blocking Ben & Jerry's from its entrepreneurial dream. Jerry handed out leaflets urging people to write in for the Ben & Jerry's "What's the Doughboy Afraid Of?" kit, which included a bumper sticker and boilerplate protest letters to the chairman of Pillsbury and the head of the Federal Trade Commission.

After a week of one-man picketing, the Associated Press picked up the story and shot it over the newswires along with a photo of Jerry picketing in front of Pillsbury with his WHAT'S THE DOUGHBOY AFRAID OF? T-shirt. A very inexpensive but highly powerful visual symbol. The press coverage began to snowball.

On the side of its ice cream containers, Ben & Jerry's promoted a toll-free hotline for the Doughboy kit. The call volume was so heavy that at the end of each day, Ben & Jerry's workers would switch from making ice cream to packing and mailing Doughboy kits. The company rented billboard space on Boston's Route 128 and advertised on Boston buses promoting the battle cry, WHAT'S THE DOUGHBOY AFRAID OF? They bought ads in *Rolling Stone* and hired airplanes to fly over Foxboro Stadium dragging banners promoting the same slogan. Ben & Jerry's didn't have a lot of money to spend, but they knew that the combination of marketing plus media was priceless.

So buzzworthy was the story that even Charlie Pillsbury, son of board member George Pillsbury, joined the crusade, sending his own letters to the Federal Trade Commission and to the chairman of Pillsbury!

Eventually, Pillsbury caved, and the press ate up the David-and-Goliath story, landing Ben & Jerry's headlines in the *New York Times,* the *Wall Street Journal,* the *Boston Globe,* the *San Francisco Chronicle;* and the AP moved the story over its wire service to newspapers and broadcast stations all across the country. A feature piece by Calvin Trillin in the July 1985 issue of *The New Yorker* recapped the whole saga. *The New Yorker* article quoted an industry expert as saying that "Ben & Jerry's accomplished in two years what would have taken 18 years using traditional means."

The American media loves a David-and-Goliath story. Americans have overcome adversity from arrival at Plymouth Rock to arrival at Ellis Island. Whether it's the American Olympic hockey team, Kiwi Airlines, or Ben & Jerry's, creating a David-and-Goliath story is a guaranteed winner.

Maxim 2: Create an Unusual or Outrageous Story to Capture the Media

Can't find a Goliath aiming to crush you?

You do have other options. Creating an unusual or outrageous story is also a tried and true winner. If the press writes about your innovative marketing, not only have you positioned your brand as innovative but you've also amplified it with the power and credibility of the press.

That's exactly what happened with Halfway, Oregon. But after you rename a town, what's next? In order to continue holding media attention, you've got to create a pipeline of ready-made unusual stories.

Examples of some oldies but goodies are the largest peanut butter and jelly sandwich in America, the biggest apple pie in America. You get the picture.

One of the ready-made unusual stories we had in our pipeline for the media was called Halfdot Comet. Literally branding a comet. We had our sound bite for the media all ready: "People keep telling us our bargains are out of this world, so that's where we went." And, "After renaming a town, there was no place to go but up!"

Thinking of it is one thing, but making it happen is another. Here's what's involved in turning such an idea into reality.

You can "buy" a comet or star online and get a certificate, but these don't have any real meaning except maybe to the person you buy one for. The International Astronomical Union (IAU) has the responsibility, and they have laid down very structured naming policies for comets.

First, a comet may be identified by the discoverer's last name (Halley's Comet, the Hale-Bopp comet). Second, comets can be named after the observatory or Sky Survey that first spots it. In fact, 90 percent of all comets are named this way. The best option was to fund an observatory and have it change its name to Halfdot Observatory, with an agreement spelled out that the next comet they reported would be named after the observatory, as Halfdot Comet.

About five or six Sky Surveys (one of them funded by the U.S. Air Force) find most comets, digitally scanning the skies with high-powered telescopes, leaving the individual astronomer with low odds of discovery.

However, the Southern Hemisphere has no Sky Surveys scanning outer space. Meaning that there's a very good chance of finding a comet if you're scanning from Australia. Ultimately the IAU has the final say on comet names. Would they follow the letter of their naming policy or not? Would it outrage the science community? Probably. Would it get immediate press? Absolutely.

I met with the codiscoverer of the Hale-Bopp comet, Alan Hale, in pursuit of this concept. We talked about the idea of renaming an observatory to "Halfdot" that would be committed to finding our comet—in exchange for funding his summer astronomy camp.

Ultimately, for reasons of timing, we ended up pushing the idea to the back burner. It's an outrageous idea still up for grabs— guaranteed to launch your brand into orbit! Visit Alan Hale's Web site at www.swisr.org if you want to go boldly where no brand has ever gone before.

Maxim 3: Create a Story of Controversy to Capture the Media

Stir up some controversy, and you've got an instant media story. Whether it be Enron, dimpled chads, or quarterback controversy on an NFL team—if it's controversial, the press will write about it.

When the teenage John McEnroe played at Wimbledon for the first time, he discovered the power of the media through controversy. Although well seeded that year, McEnroe was relatively un-known in world tennis. Frustrated with his own play during a match at Wimbledon, he sent his racket careening across the court.

The crowd reacted immediately with a combination of boos and gasps.

McEnroe realized that, much to his surprise, he had the crowd in the palm of his hand. Intrigued, he thought he might try it again to see if he could evoke the same response.

He tried it again. Sure enough, they reacted even more. More boos, more horrified gasps. That night, he was on a plane to the United States, unaware the British press had branded him the Bad Boy of tennis in its headlines. When he got off the plane, the previously unknown teenager was amazed at the flurry of press attention and his new headline status.

A few moments of playful controversy created McEnroe's new image and a media storm. He rode it for all it was worth and played out the role of bad boy to the fullest extent.

Look at the difference between two tennis players: Pete Sampras and John McEnroe. Both are excellent players, but McEnroe captured the attention of the media. McEnroe gets buzz that Sampras can't touch.

Stir up some controversy, and the media will follow. Stir up controversy by design, and you could get McEnroe-style buzz.

Maxim 4: Create a Celebrity Story

How much would you expect to pay for a used Lexus with about ninety thousand miles, and a Blue Book value of around $9,000? About $9,000, right?

Not if the vehicle happened to have belonged to Bill Gates. In that case, the selling price was $38,000, or about four times its book value.

America has a fascination with celebrities. What cars are they driving? What clothes are they wearing to the Oscars? Entire sections of newspapers are dedicated to celebrities. *MTV Cribs* is the modern day version of *Lifestyles of the Rich & Famous.* And then there's *People* magazine, *Access Hollywood,* and other media venues that are solely devoted to celebrities. Celebrities get instant media attention.

What's the impact of celebrity buzz? If used the right way, it can be huge.

CELEBRITY STORIES, EXAMPLE 1: GAME READY

CoolSystems, Inc., developed a product that reduces the recovery time of athletic injuries. Imagine a linebacker whose injury is scheduled to keep him out for two weeks—and then cut that recovery time in half with the Game Ready product.

Sprained ankle, jammed wrist, injured shoulder, or twisted knee, Game Ready is ready. A form-fitting neoprene wrap uses NASA spacesuit technology that runs chilled water through the wraps (avoiding freeze burn or water mess); it alternately compresses for several minutes, then relaxes for several minutes. Real healing can't start until the swelling is completely gone, and no other treatment rivals the patented Game Ready product. But it isn't cheap, retailing for more than $2,000.

An early start-up in 1998, Game Ready in 2005 boasts more than $4 million annual revenues with just eight employees. Today, more than 125 NFL players on twenty-three NFL teams use the product. More than forty-two NBA players on sixteen NBA teams use the product, as do the Navy Seals, several Olympic athletes, and more than sixty-eight NCAA college teams. But as with any start-up, success takes time, the right product, the right plan, and buzz.

How did Game Ready get buzz?

First and foremost, it knew it had to deliver a product that worked. In the beginning, like most beta versions (trial versions) of products, it was on the right track but not really working yet. Game Ready searched for the right engineers to continue perfecting it, and worked closely with the U.S. Olympic Training Center in Colorado as its testing ground. With a lot of effort, Game Ready was finally ready.

It may have required some rocket science to engineer the product, but it didn't take a rocket scientist to figure out the primary market. There are only twenty-eight NFL teams, but there are thousands of college sports programs. Ultimately, Game Ready would make its money in the college market. But thinking smart, Game Ready made sports celebrities one of its key components to create buzz and capture the media. It knew the power of celebrity influence—if it was good enough for the New York Yankees, it must be good enough for Notre Dame (both now have players using the product).

Conventional marketing wisdom would say, "Sign up the biggest sports celebrities you can find, and put them in ads." And then you're all set, right? Not quite. Consider this: Tiger Woods— perhaps the jewel of all sports celebs to endorse a product—signed a $105 million endorsement deal with Nike. When Tiger's game went south, he switched away from his Nike driver back to Titleist. Rolex spent an ocean full of money getting Tiger to wear and endorse Rolex watches. When the Rolex contract was up, Tiger switched to rival TAG Heuer for a $6 million contract. Tiger will probably be wearing a Timex in due time. Kobe Bryant, he's an Adidas man to the bone . . . well, er, until Nike signed him to a $40 million-plus contract.

Endorsements used to create lasting value. NASCAR would like you to believe the fans who come out to its races or watch them on television will buy more of your product because of a logo on a hood. Wonder why Winston dropped its title sponsorship of NASCAR's Winston Cup? Because mindless logo slapping doesn't work, that's why.

But the bottom line today is: Consumers are wiser than ever before. They know that endorsements are not based on the best product, but the highest bidder. Martina Hingis signed up with tennis shoe company Sergio Tacchini for $5.6 million, and she later sued the company because the shoes hurt her feet.

And Game Ready's marketers under Gabriel Griego, the company's director of marketing, knew this all too well. He came from humble roots, no fancy endorsements, and lots of buzz: He had been marketing PowerBar. The secrets that Gabe Griego learned at PowerBar translated to Game Ready.

How do you build a brand from nothing to a well-known, respected, and profitable brand? Generally speaking, you flip the marketing model upside down. Most marketing models start with traditional first, then word of mouth and buzz second (if at all). PowerBar was built on word-of-mouth buzz first, and only later did it add in traditional marketing (print ads, etc). PowerBar's board requested countless analyses from Griego, trying to pinpoint its marketing success, and there was no single thing that produced correlation. Gabe Griego measured success by word of mouth. If people came up to him at events or at a backyard barbeque and started talking about PowerBar, he knew it was working. If people didn't talk about a specific marketing effort, he would drop it.

One thing people talk about a lot in the world of sports is professional athletes. Griego knew the key to getting buzz for Game Ready would be professional athletes. Now getting a pro athlete on the phone isn't easy; getting a strength training coach or physical therapist for a professional team on the phone is a lot easier. Strength training coaches and therapists are influencers holding a lot of weight in the world of pro sports. They help prevent injuries and help heal injuries. And injuries can be the only thing separating an athlete from a paycheck and a contract.

The company came up with this game plan:

Tactic 1: Solicit real input and feedback from strength coaches and therapists in order to refine the product in the hope that they'll offer it as a solution to their team's professional athletes.

Tactic 2: Do *not* give the product away for free. Make everyone pay. Countless times a professional athlete would call the CEO of Game Ready, asking for a free unit. Without exception, every athlete was made to pay. Consumers today can smell an ad a mile away, and they're pretty savvy. Making multimillion-dollar pro athletes pay for the product without exception establishes product authenticity. If a celebrity chooses to use a product on his or her own instead of being given it free, the honesty and authenticity speaks volumes.

Tactic 3: Establish confidence and a quiet relationship with pro athletes. Speaking with people of celebrity status is delicate. Everyone is looking for something from them—an autograph, a favor, or just a glimpse. Most companies with access would ask for permission to use a photo, or an endorsement. Game Ready made it a point not to do this.

Tactic 4: Once celebrity athletes are actively using the product, they effectively endorse it through their own choice. Then Game Ready leverages those "endorsements" with other professional athletes. When a personal trainer for one of the New York Yankees players was approached to use Game Ready, the trainer balked. But the next day, he saw a private list of all the pro athletes using the product. That was enough: The first New York Yankee ballplayer started using it immediately. As P. T. Barnum said, "There's nothing that attracts a crowd like a crowd." But with a crowd of celebrities, you not only attract a larger crowd—you also attract the media.

Tactic 5: Leverage the media. Once Game Ready got a crowd of sports celebrities using the product, it began to tell its story to the media. Using empirical data (cutting recovery time by about half) combined with sports celebrities using the product, it seeded the story of Game Ready being the "unfair advantage" in sports. It didn't go to *People* magazine but stayed with the plan of influencing the influencers (strength coaches, personal trainers, and physical therapists) and pitched the story to nondescript publications in that niche and to local sportswriters.

When reporters asked which professional teams and athletes were using the product, Game Ready simply pointed the media to the teams or the athletes themselves. With established relationships and the authenticity of the product, sports celebrities would often speak to the media. In turn, Game Ready would leverage quotes from local publications, ABC, and CBS.

Famous sports agent Leigh Steinberg now sits on the board of directors of the company, and the celebrity factor continues to grow. What sports celebs are next in line for Game Ready? Surprisingly, the answer even includes a kind of "athlete" you might not think of: next year's Smarty Jones and just about every other thoroughbred race horse that's a Triple Crown contender. In the horse racing business, horse's knees take a beating and often need ice and compression, but water dribbling on a horse's hoofs poses a problem. Enter Game Ready designed for horses, at $4,000 per unit, and it becomes equine bling bling. As word-of-mouth news spread to the equine market, Game Ready was taking orders before the first production unit was ready.

Look for it on TV as more horses, halfbacks, and southpaws wear a Game Ready.

Celebrity Stories, Example 2: Wolford and Perhaps You

For Wolford America, celebrity media attention boosted sales by a factor of ten. Wolford's fishnet stockings ($35 retail price) were included inside the gift bags for the 2000 Oscar attendees, and Cameron Diaz also chose to wear them to the opening of *Charlie's Angels*. Sales took off. Ten times higher than pre-Oscar levels.

But because of such stories, you're starting to see massive clutter in celebrity goody bags. Instead of a manageable shopping bag, goody bags have exploded to the size of massive duffel bags, and it just doesn't work as well. So how might you capitalize on celebrity buzz?

Combine celebrity news with any of the other most frequently written news stories—something unusual, something controversial, something newsworthy. When you start combing two or three of the five most frequently written news stories, you really capture the media.

I helped an Internet client—Screensavers.com, a division of Miva—climb from 450,000 visitors a month to more than ten million using this exact strategy. When teen stars Lindsay Lohan and Hilary Duff surfaced, Screensavers.com was right there to offer pop-culture pulse data on who would be the new "it" girl (answer: Lohan). When the media was abuzz about *Queer Eye for the Straight Guy,* Screensavers.com was there to declare "they've been Osbourned" as it saw their screensaver downloads decline. Janet Jackson, William Hung, Martha Stewart, Ashlee Simpson, Heidi Klum, Spider-Man, David Beckham, and Olympian Michael Phelps trends all keep the celebrity buzz machine going for Screensavers .com again and again to the point where it's been touted as the "pop culture pulse taker" by the *Los Angeles Times.*

More on How to Use Celebrities for Buzz

If I were running Hooked-on-Phonics, how would I create buzz? Pitch Dan Quayle to be my spokesperson, of course. If I were running Tylenol, I'd solicit Troy Aikman (or any other concussion-laden quarterback) to pitch my product. If I were marketing Ginsu Knives, pitchman John Wayne Bobbitt would surely be my pick. The point? You may not need them to actually endorse your product (although it might be worth the money at a fair price) . . . but the audacity of conceiving and pitching such an idea alone is news-worthy enough to capture media attention. ("Kitchen Knife Company Seeks John Wayne Bobbitt as Spokesman." Can't you just see that headline in mainstream newspapers?)

But what about if you're with a really, really small company? Can you still get celebrity buzz?

It depends. Quite often you've got to combine two or more of the five most frequently written news stories. Most of my clients tend to be mid- to large-size companies, but occasionally I take on clients much smaller. Jesse Keller, CEO of PersonalsTrainer.com, had sold his prior company to Korn/Ferry for $30 million. After PersonalsTrainer was up and running for nine months, it hadn't gotten an iota of press. He came to us for help, and a week later, we had Jesse talking to the *Wall Street Journal.* We got PersonalsTrainer .com on the coveted "A-head" spot on page one of the *Journal,* and the media and servers started buzzing.

Jesse had two of the most frequently written news stories waiting to be tapped. First, an unusual business model. Literally thousands of people use online dating services like match.com, but because of competition and clutter, a lot of the customers of those sites never get dating inquiries. So PersonalsTrainer will tune up your dating profile, rewriting your description, advising you on your photo, and providing general advice—all for under $250.

But the real secret to the success we brought him was what we call the pseudo-celebrity angle. The interesting twist to PersonalsTrainer is that the writers from HBO's *Sex and the City* and from Discovery Channel's *Extreme Dating* are the ones rewriting your profile and advising you! Don't have the resources to sign Kim Cattrall or Sarah Jessica Parker as a spokesperson? Recruit the writers who created their celebrity characters! Pseudo-celebrities can sometimes be just as good as celebrities themselves.

We packed together two of the most frequently written news stories together, and captured attention on page one of the most influential business newspaper in America.

Maxim 5: Create a Story That's Already Hot in the Media

Ever heard the term media frenzy? An abundance of journalists get their information from other news stories. All too often, the media follows the fire. If a topic gets hot in the press, it gets even hotter. Editors and reporters want to scoop their competition with new angles on a hot story, and the frenzy perpetuates itself.

Just remember these stories: Enron, Gary Condit, dimpled chads, Elián Gonzalez, California rolling blackouts, stem cell research, cloning, Monica Lewinsky, JonBenét Ramsey, O.J., Whitewater, Laci Peterson, the Governator Arnold Schwarzenegger, Martha Stewart. The press has a tendency to fuel itself and pour even more gasoline on a story.

If you want to capture the media, create a story that piggybacks on hot topics they're already covering.

One of the best examples of piggybacking is the premise of Bill Clinton's first presidential campaign, a premise engineered by James Carville. At the time, the Gulf War was over, there was lots going on in the country and the world, but it seemed as if almost the only thing the press was writing about was the suffering economy. Knowing that this was already the hottest topic in the media, Carville created the headline, which later became famous, "It's the economy, stupid!"

So what do you do if you've got an everyday brand trying to ride the wave of existing media? If you're Pringles Potato Chips, and George Bush just choked on a pretzel, create a national radio spot promoting the lifesaving antidote of Pringles (using a Bush impersonator voice). If you're Kentucky Fried Chicken and Oprah's being dragged into court with Texas cattlemen in a beef debate, create the Texas Cattle Tuesday special! If you're Home Depot and what's hot in the media is the Pentagon buying toilet seats for $500, advertise Home Depot's low-priced toilet seats versus the Pentagon's. If you're Monster.com and Donald Trump's *The Apprentice* is hot in the media, run a temporary campaign, "You're Hired." If you can capitalize on an existing frenzy, do so. You'll capture the media, and get buzz.

A Devil's Advocate Summary

So you're a marketing person. You say, "That's for the PR folks— it's got nothing to do with me in marketing." Oh, but it's got everything to do with you.

Keep marketing (capturing consumer attention) and PR (capturing media attention) separate in your organization, and it will be the biggest mistake you can make. Why?

Because media already *has* consumer attention. Remember that people, including your consumers, purchase *Time* magazine not for the advertising but for the articles. The media can create a buzz for you, increasing the effectiveness of your existing marketing dollars sixfold. Capture media attention and that's great. But combine marketing with captured media attention and that's priceless. Combine it! Leverage it!

Align the people in your organization to create marketing and capture the media together. If they don't get along, replace them. Marketing plus media is priceless.

So you're thinking, "I don't know, I think we should just stick to the normal approach of issuing a press release. After all, we've got our new 3.2 version coming out next month."

Earth to emperor. Earth to emperor. Please find mirror and place clothes on body.

Sometimes what's news to you, simply isn't news. Consult a journalist or ask a PR professional who's got some history in the business (and not looking to get more business). Honest professionals will tell you what's really news.

Keep in mind those five most frequently written news stories that are tried and true. As a simple test, ask yourself:

- Is there a David-and-Goliath story here? (Be honest.)
- Is there something unusual or outrageous here? (Be honest.)
- Is there a dramatic story of controversy here? (Be honest.)
- Is there a celebrity angle? (Be honest.)
- Is this really a story that's already hot in the news? (Again, be honest.)

Stick with the five most frequently written stories, and discover how to increase the effectiveness of your marketing budget sixfold.

CHAPTER EIGHT

Apple Mac Attack: What Few Know

In 1982, the best-selling desktop computer wasn't from IBM. And it wasn't from Apple. The best-selling computer in 1982 was the Commodore 64. Apple turned that around with a new product and a memorable TV commercial; many know the story but few know the buzz backstory.

Apple was enjoying sales close to the Commodore's but just hanging on, unable to gain an edge. Until that historic year of 1984, when Apple took off with breakaway sales. Maybe you remember the event that marked the beginning of the startling rise for Apple. One little television commercial, released on January 22, 1984, announcing the company's newest, most innovative computer—the Macintosh.

That commercial changed history not only for Apple Computer but for the entire advertising industry.

The Good and the Bad

An interesting twist to Apple's marketing success beginning in 1984 was its effort with another new computer, the Lisa, which was introduced just before the Macintosh but crash-landed. Both computers were launched with TV commercials directed by film mogul Ridley Scott (director of blockbuster film spectaculars including *Gladiator, Blade Runner,* and *Alien*).

The commercial for the Lisa computer that launched in late 1983 fell flat. No one wrote about it, no one talked about it. Quite simply, it failed miserably.

The commercials for the Lisa and the Macintosh were similar in style and cinematography and were both directed by Ridley Scott. Why did one fail and one succeed? The story provides some valuable lessons in buzz.

One of These Things Is Not Like the Other

Nearly midway through 1983, a group of people from Apple and from their ad agency, Chiat/Day, sat around a conference room table devising plans for the launch of the Macintosh.

The launch date for the Mac had originally been set for June 1983, but technical delays pushed that date to early the following year: 1984. Maybe it was inevitable that someone would think of the connection with the famous George Orwell novel *Nineteen Eighty-Four,* with its memorable Big Brother theme. The decision had been made: The commercial would be a take-off on Big Brother.

The original intention was to air the commercial January 1, 1984, on all the TV College Bowl games. As it turned out, the expense of the Bowl games proved too costly for Apple. So they settled on launching Macintosh on what, at the time, was a cheaper media alternative: the Super Bowl. (Hard to picture, but in those days the Super Bowl wasn't the platform it is today, and would morph into America's premiere ad event only because of the buzz created by Apple.)

In December 1983, the final version of what has come to be

called the 1984 commercial was ready, and was screened for Apple's board of directors.

The board hated it. The look and feel reminded them of the Lisa commercial that hadn't done the job of putting that computer on the map. Even CEO John Sculley shied away from it because it wasn't the conventional lifestyle genre of advertising he preferred.

The only supporters of the 1984 commercial were Steve Jobs and Floyd Kvamme, who had showed it to Apple's entire sales force several weeks earlier in Hawaii. The sales force had gone ballistic with enthusiasm; Jobs and Kvamme knew they had a winner on their hands.

But the board was gun-shy. They ordered Floyd Kvamme to sell all the airtime bought for the Super Bowl and abandon the 1984 commercial. Apple's 1984 commercial was dead; it would never be seen by the American public.

Dutifully following the board's directive, Kvamme ordered the Super Bowl airtime to be sold. They managed to sell everything except for one last sixty-second block.

Late one Friday afternoon, Kvamme and his right-hand man, Bill Campbell, got a phone call. An offer for the last sixty seconds came in at $700,000—Apple had paid $900,000. It was a pivotal moment that would change Apple forever. The executive vice president of marketing and sales for Apple looked at his right-hand man and said, "We never got this call." The last sixty seconds of airtime were kept, and the 1984 commercial aired January 22, 1984.

The words "We never got this call" were about as close to insubordination as Floyd Kvamme ever got. That one decision may have changed the course of Apple.

But therein lies the rub. Creating buzz comes with a certain amount of risk. And risk is something that boards of directors rarely want to take. Creating successful buzz is always uncomfortable and always unconventional.

Buzz foresight is never clear, buzz hindsight is always 20/20.

The Commercial

Because Super Bowl Sunday wasn't until late in January, Kvamme and Chiat/Day were deathly afraid that someone else would create a commercial using the same Orwellian theme before the Apple commercial aired. They knew they didn't have a monopoly on good ideas, and the connection between the calendar year 1984 and the Orwell book of that name was too obvious to miss.

On January first, Kvamme, Campbell, and the Chiat/Day team spent all day surfing College Bowl games, looking for an Orwellian ad. They breathed a sigh of relief to discover that there were none to be seen.

Twenty-two days went by too slowly. Finally, it was time for the Super Bowl.

The game was a blowout, but fans stayed tuned in in hopes of a comeback. Halftime came and went. Early in the third quarter, a touchdown provided the opportunity for a commercial break. Television screens all across America faded to black, and then Apple's 1984 commercial faded in.

The commercial begins with an athletic blond woman clad in bright red shorts and a white Apple T-shirt. Chased by storm troopers, she bursts into an auditorium where a Hitler-like event is taking place. Rows of drones with shaved heads sit motionless, devoid of life, as an image of Big Brother spews authoritarian diatribe from a huge overhead screen at the front of the auditorium. The blonde runs toward the screen and hurls a sledgehammer at the image of Big Brother. The screen explodes as the sledgehammer crashes into it. A voice is then heard: "On January 24th, Apple Computer will introduce Macintosh. And you'll see why 1984 won't be like *Nineteen Eighty-Four*."

Immediately, phones lit up at local TV stations across the country. People asked, "What was that?" and requested that their station run it again so they could take another look. Apple Computer's phone lines started ringing. CBS headquarters' phone lines started ringing. The media replayed the commercial on every national network and on hundreds of local TV stations. The football game was a nonstory, a 38–9 rout. The real media story was Apple's 1984 commercial that took the nation by storm.

What created even more buzz was Apple's outrageous declaration that the sixty-second commercial that had cost nearly $1 million to produce, would never be aired again. Apple was throwing away a valuable piece of advertising worth $1 million dollars!

The truth was that the company just didn't have any more money in the budget to air the spot again. But Steve Jobs and his people wisely didn't disclose the real reason. The seemingly outrageous decision to throw away the $1 million ad created an air of exclusivity that piqued the interest of the public and the press even more. Because Apple wouldn't be running it again, the commercial was replayed on networks and local TV stations time and time again. Millions of dollars of airtime and zero cost to the company. Incredible.

Dissecting the Buzz

The Lisa commercial didn't get people talking. It didn't create buzz.

The 1984 commercial had four key ingredients of buzz that the Lisa commercial didn't have:

- Hot topic in the media
- Controversy
- David vs. Goliath
- The unusual

The first ingredient played on the George Orwell novel. Written soon after World War II, in the late 1940s, the book had a prediction that was an uneasy one: In the year 1984, we would lose control of our lives and our individual spirit. An authoritarian Big

Brother would control every aspect of our lives. The Apple commercial connected with a hot topic already in the press, and a hot topic already in popular culture.

The second key ingredient of buzz success was controversy. The press, of course, feeds on controversy, and the 1984 commercial provided plenty. In an October 1983 edition of *Business Week* magazine, a writer claimed that "the battle for market supremacy is suddenly all over, and IBM is the winner . . . industry watchers predict IBM will account for half the world market." But it wasn't to be that way.

Without actually mentioning IBM, Apple cleverly disguised Big Brother as IBM (which was nicknamed Big Blue). The commercial dramatized the parallel of personal computers versus mainframes, pitting the individual freedom of Apple against the overbearing control of Big Blue.

The third ingredient of buzz success was the David-and-Goliath story. Big Brother and Big Blue both represented a Goliath. The lone attacker hurling the sledgehammer was a lady in the role of David.

The fourth ingredient of success that created buzz for Apple's 1984 commercial was its unusual nature. A single sixty-second TV spot was unusual, and so was its extraordinarily high million-dollar production cost. But even more unusual was Apple's declaration that the expensive, sixty-second commercial would never be aired again. The decision to throw away a million-dollar commercial created exclusivity, which piqued the interest of the public and the press, heightening the buzz.

And what did that commercial mean in terms of sales? Recall that Apple had been running neck and neck with Commodore since 1980. The following graph shows what happened in the decade following the ingenious commercial—a powerful demonstration of the power of buzz.

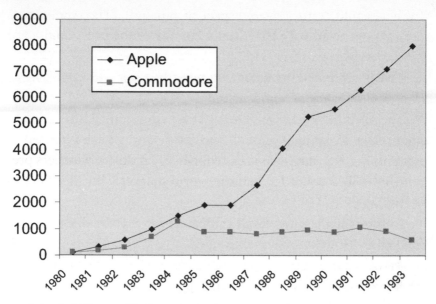

Sales in Millions of Dollars, Apple Computer vs. Commodore Computers
(SOURCE: ANNUAL REPORTS OF THE TWO COMPANIES)

Payoff for the Super Bowl

Back in 1984, the Super Bowl was not known as an event to showcase a new ad campaign. But Apple played its hand so well—especially with the news of never replaying the commercial—that the day after the Super Bowl Americans were talking about advertising. Apple's advertising started conversations, and its buzz became the envy of every advertiser.

In 1985, a herd of advertisers stampeded into Super Bowl ads, trying to capture some of the same magical buzz. The Super Bowl became America's number-one advertising event. It's now the beauty pageant of the advertising industry, where agencies put forth their best work. No other day rivals the attention now devoted to Super Bowl advertising, thanks to Apple's buzz.

A Story That Can't Be Repeated?

Apple is a story of a brand that created buzz in 1984, and broke away from its pack of competitors.

The skeptic in you might say, "That was another time and another place. Creating buzz and breakaway growth can't happen in tough industries like the computer industry today. Just look at the industry now!"

Bull puckey.

Even in tough industries, if you create buzz, you can experience breakaway growth.

In Salt Lake City, there's a computer manufacturer creating buzz, kicking butt, and taking names. It's Totally Awesome. Literally—Totally Awesome Computers.

When I tell people about Totally Awesome Computers, they ask me, "Is there any growth *left* in that industry?" Totally Awesome is bucking the trend, creating buzz, and experiencing breakaway growth. Here's how.

Built from the Ground Up on Buzz

In 1996, a man named Dell Schanze sold a computer that he had built himself. He began building and selling more but was finding enough customers to do only about five a month. So he decided to try some marketing.

He walked into a radio station, bought some AM radio time, and made his own commercial. A month after his radio campaign, he went from selling five computers a month to forty-eight computers a month.

But this wasn't your everyday radio commercial. In fact, it didn't sound like a radio commercial at all. It just sounded like a guy talking about weird stuff . . . and that's what it was. He's never stopped. You hear one of his radio commercials, and he's talking about life. Or he's talking about family values, marriage, and God. He borders on the outrageous. In one of his radio commercials, he's even French-kissing his dog!

The French-kiss commercial astounded radio listeners and prompted a flood of complaints. But guess what? That week was also his best in sales. He creates buzz.

He also talks about the competition. Making remarks about business ethics, he'll mention how Circuit City charges a huge re-stocking fee if you're not satisfied with a computer purchase. How Bill Gates doesn't love his customers the way that Dell Schanze does. He trashes Dell and Gateway because he bench tests his product against theirs and has the data to prove that his computer is far superior. (Dell and Gateway have both sent legal notices, but haven't been able to muzzle him.)

He's so confident in the quality of his product that he offers $1,000 to anyone who can show him bench-test results proving there's a better PC out there than Totally Awesome's.

But many advertising experts claim that Totally Awesome has it all wrong. Dell Schanze doesn't know what advertising is. He doesn't know what branding is. He's making it up as he goes along.

Yes, he is. But it works.

Why? First, his advertising doesn't sound like advertising. Usually when people hear commercials, they stop listening. But people who write him letters claim they look forward to every new commercial of his (there's a new set every week), and that it's inspirational. For Dell Schanze, the purpose of his advertising is not to sell stuff—it's to have fun.

His marketing philosophy is contrarian but simple. The more you shout, "Buy stuff from us, buy stuff from us!" the more people push their big *Ignore* button. They stop paying attention to your advertising.

Innocently enough, the real secret is that he's *not* creating advertising, he's creating content. Content that entertains. And guess what? People pay far more attention to entertaining content than they do advertising. Dell Schanze from Totally Awesome might be a little crazy, but he's the farthest thing from Crazy Eddie. He speaks the truth (except when kidding that he's going to fire Bill Gates for being lame). He's unpredictable and unexpected. He creates buzz because he's outrageous, he's unusual, and he's the David fighting Goliath (even though he views himself as Goliath due to his high ethical standards, service standards, and product standards).

He's come a long way from that first-month advertising on radio, when he spent $900 and sold forty-eight computers. Now he spends $54,000 a month on advertising and sells $2 million to $3 million worth of computers. Yet even with such an increase in advertising, his biggest source of customers is still word of mouth. Three-quarters of his customers come from word of mouth. And word-of-mouth marketing is the most powerful form of marketing on earth.

His message has spread far and wide. He boasts word-of-mouth customers from Alaska to Hawaii to Alabama—and he doesn't advertise in *any* of those states!

Dell Schanze creates buzz and markets with buzz.

People have been misled and lied to by thousands of advertisers. Perhaps they've ruined it for most of us—who knows? But what Dell Schanze knows is this: People want honesty in advertising, people want entertainment, and people want creative content.

Even in tough industries, you can experience the same breakaway growth as Totally Awesome Computers. All you need is buzz.

CHAPTER NINE

ClearPlay: Courts, Controversy, and Clamor

Capturing media attention involves much more than creating buzz-worthy ads. In fact, buzzmarketing can be 100 percent ad-less.

So what road does a CEO follow when he's committed to buzzmarketing and his investors don't get it? If you were Bill Aho, the CEO of start-up company ClearPlay, you'd listen.

The investors, in all their wisdom, argued that an up-and-coming outfit had to have some "real marketing." They believed in tradition. They believed in duplicating the exact same plans of most big brands that spend millions and millions of dollars in marketing. They thought they had the solution. A full-page ad in the *Wall Street Journal* trumpeting the arrival of ClearPlay. The ad ran and they waited for their stock to take off.

And waited and waited . . .

I've heard similar stories again, and again, and again. I've had clients excitedly show me the imposing ad they were about to run in publications even more important than the *Wall Street Journal,* hoping for great results. I wince, and diplomatically suggest it won't work. Money pours down the drain. Lambs continue to follow the herd. On their way to slaughter.

It's the radio campaign aired on Howard Stern. It's the expensive ad during the NBA finals. Substitute the names, and I'm sure you've heard the same stories. The answers are the same. Nothing really happens. A waste of dollars. I have many smart friends who have made this mistake, and I confess I've made this mistake myself.

Some will tell you it's a frequency thing. You need to spend *more* money to see results. Don't believe the hype.

After seeing the disappointing results of their full page *Wall Street Journal* ad, ClearPlay's investors faced the music. Not much happened. A lot of money wasted. The ClearPlay CEO knew in the back of his mind it wouldn't work. But the investors had been so convinced it would work that they paid for the ad themselves. Sure, that money could have been put to more effective use elsewhere, but when other people pay, you don't say no. No such "real marketing" efforts were undertaken again.

So what is ClearPlay and how did it get buzz?

The Filtering Product

Our entertainment today comes loaded with images and language that used to be for the locker room and the barroom—and unacceptable anywhere else. And while many people take it all in stride, many others don't—not just as a matter of protecting the young'uns. They themselves feel assaulted by what to them is too much swearing, sex, and violence, and choose to live in a more pure world.

For a lot of folks, though, this presents a dilemma: They miss seeing many highly praised films that everybody else is talking about. It just doesn't seem fair.

ClearPlay offers a solution: a ClearPlay-enabled DVD player can be programmed by the user so the family can watch movies in a whole new way. Offering a variety of options, it allows the user to filter out any combination of graphic violence, full nudity, partial nudity, crude language, explicit drug use, ethnic and social slurs, and so on—in all, offering fourteen different filtering categories to choose from.

The Unseen Competitors

The saying that there's nothing new under the sun doesn't seem to be valid these days; there seem to be brilliant new inventions everywhere we look. Unfortunately, the trash-free DVD enabler isn't one of them. Or, rather, the idea may be relatively new, but ClearPlay isn't the only one that has it. The marketplace has already gathered shoulder-to-shoulder competitors with names like CleanFlicks, MovieMask, Movie Shield Box, and Clean Films.

But they are nowhere to be found on the radar screen. Not one of them has any "mind share" among the public. No one knows about them, no one talks about them, no one writes about them. The field was open for one of the competitors to break out from the crowd and make its presence known. ClearPlay was the one that broke out.

People talk about them, the media writes about them, celebrity movie directors like Steven Spielberg and Martin Scorsese feel threatened by them, congressmen and senators have hearings about them, and Wal-Mart now sells ClearPlay-enabled DVD players in a majority of its stores.

Demand for the Product

Ever noticed how many inventions seem to be the outgrowth of some individual's annoyance or frustration in his own life? ClearPlay was born from just such a frustration, sprouting from the brain of founder Matt Jarman. Several plain facts supported the concept.

When consulting firm Paul Kagen Associates studied a decade of the movie industry, they found that 3 percent of theatrical feature films accounted for 50 percent of the entire movie industry's profits. And those films were G-rated! R-rated movies represented only 12 percent of the industry's profits—even though most of the theatrical feature films made in Hollywood these days carry an R rating; in 2003, the figure was 81 percent.

It seemed pretty basic. The market for family entertainment yields huge profits, yet has a tiny supply. Huge demand, tiny supply equals good opportunity.

I'm familiar with the situation myself, as the proud parent of an eleven-year-old and two toddlers. For myself, am I fine with seeing Janet Jackson's breast on TV? No complaints. But am I fine with my kids seeing Janet Jackson's breast on TV? No. I'm by no means a prude, but there are certain things I want to protect my kids from seeing until they're older.

If, like me, you have kids of varied ages, you know the problem gets even stickier. When my daughter becomes nineteen, my son will be nine. I love the idea of being able to filter out stuff for the nine-year-old, so all of us can watch. ClearPlay lets me do that.

The product itself is smoother than the dubbed, made-for-TV versions of movies. At thirty frames a second with DVD digital technology, Jim Carrey's middle finger is smoothly erased from *Bruce Almighty,* Governor Arnold Schwarzenegger's naked butt is smoothly skipped from *Terminator 3,* and Meg Ryan's orgasm scene in *When Harry Met Sally* is given the heave-ho.

A Fork in the Business . . . a Fork in the Road

After starting the company in 1997, ClearPlay began its long journey of transforming an idea into reality. Through several twists and turns, it got a break. ClearPlay was negotiating a deal with Sanyo, which had agreed to make their next DVD player with the ClearPlay standard.

ClearPlay management had been courting investors and courting Wal-Mart at the same time. With some research in hand from the well-respected Wirthlin Group (they helped reposition brands like McDonald's and helped get Ronald Reagan elected), ClearPlay learned that 63 percent of Americans were "interested" or "very interested" in the ability to filter out certain content from movies. More interesting was the fact that the response wasn't confined to specific regions or types of communities. Heavily populated religious areas (the South, Salt Lake City) didn't really differ from areas like New York, Boston, or Los Angeles. Parents are parents wherever you go.

Wal-Mart dug the concept, Sanyo dug the concept. DVD processors were designed, working prototypes were completed. The first Sanyo production run was four days away.

And then on September 20, 2002, it hit the fan.

Steven Spielberg, Martin Scorsese, and twelve other directors—the entertainment industry's movie director elite, represented by the Hollywood-based Director's Guild of America (DGA)—were about to sue every player in the filtering industry for copyright infringement. In essence they were saying, "Alter our movies in any way and you're tampering with artistic integrity, and we'll come after you with a vengeance." And that's exactly what they were doing.

One of ClearPlay's competitors, CleanFlicks, discovered the Hollywood directors' planned lawsuit and proactively sued the DGA for declaratory judgment. In turn, the Hollywood elite sent out for reinforcements. They convinced eight major movie studios to join them in the lawsuit and to expand the offense by counter-suing even more players filtering explicit movie content.

As it turned out, ClearPlay wasn't big enough to be considered in the initial DGA suit. The action focused on the big fish of the industry, and ClearPlay was, at the time, a minnow. Things looked great. For a while.

Only when Hollywood filed its counterclaims was every single player in the filtering industry named, including ClearPlay. When the sheriff arrived on CEO Bill Aho's doorstep serving a lawsuit from some of the biggest money-making movie studios in America—he knew only three months into his job that things were getting rough.

They got rougher.

Upon hearing the news of Hollywood's suing ClearPlay and the entire industry, Sanyo's lawyers got nervous and thought it, too, would be named in the suit. The company didn't feel like fighting eight studios and fourteen directors, and they bailed. No DVD players with ClearPlay functionality would be made by Sanyo.

ClearPlay was in a deep bind. And so close: The first units would have been coming off the line in just a few weeks. Without a DVD manufacturer, no ClearPlay DVD filters would be sold; and, of course, the juicy, lucrative Wal-Mart opportunity would evaporate as well. The long road to finding a manufacturer would have to begin all over again.

Decision Time

Bill Aho knew he had an opportunity. Most CEOs would cringe at the thought of being sued by eight movie studios and wealthy directors like Steven Spielberg, a man who makes more in three months than Aho had made in his entire life. But Aho understood the fundamentals of buzz.

Controversy makes a good news story. Every reporter loves a ripe David-vs.-Goliath brouhaha (as we saw in "The Second Secret—Capture Media"). He knew he had the ingredients of buzz and innately understood that buzz was a much better way to launch a brand than with advertising.

A fork in the road. CEO Aho faced two choices: Avoid the controversy, play it low-key, and keep legal costs to a minimum. Or go from an unrecognized industry player to the industry leader and a lightning rod for Hollywood's wrath, bearing the legal costs for the industry almost entirely on his company's shoulders.

Aho chose the latter. Yes, it would be expensive. Yes, they would have to withstand bolts of legal lightning from Hollywood lawyers. But it was also an opportunity to get people talking about the ClearPlay brand, and get the media writing about the ClearPlay brand. Just like Apple in 1984, it was time to take risks—a financial risk, a personal risk. Aho saw the opportunity and consciously made the decision to take the lead role and fight the entire entertainment industry.

Imagine proposing a marketing budget devoted entirely to legal fees. That's what ClearPlay went for: a marketing budget not devoted to advertising but to keeping its attorneys in cigars and caviar. Unconventional and risky, yes. Most executives would be fired.

But a funny common denominator to buzz is this: In foresight, it's viewed as ludicrous. In hindsight, it's viewed as brilliant.

Bring It On!

While thirteen other filtering competitors ran scared (and some ran for the woods), no-name ClearPlay took up the challenge. It broke away from the other companies named in the lawsuits and began its own legal battle.

Legal motions from ClearPlay shot across the bow of the big-name directors in Hollywood fashion—dramatic and confident. The media picked up the story and focused on the little guy fighting back. It's a picture-perfect story to capture the media (an example of both the story of controversy and the David-vs.-Goliath story). Resources, the company didn't have a lot. Spunk, soul, and smarts—it had truckloads.

In early 2003, the media frenzy begins. It becomes the hottest topic in intellectual property law, and the hottest intellectual property law firms start courting ClearPlay to be its legal counsel. The case has all the makings of legal stardom. Taking on eight movie studios and fourteen of Hollywood's elite directors. Combine the earnings of all, and you're going up against an entity exceeding the gross domestic product of most third-world countries. But precedents in this area, of law are few. The attorney who could play in this area, combining the new technology developed by ClearPlay with the egos of Hollywood celebrities, could catapult a workaday attorney into Johnnie Cochran or Mark Geragos status.

Attorney Andrew Bridges came to ClearPlay with impeccable credentials stemming most recently from his success representing Diamond Multimedia, makers of the popular MP3 player called Rio, against the Recording Industry Association of America (RIAA), part of the music industry's reaction in fear of youngsters ripping it off by bootleg downloads from the Napster and Kazaa Web sites. Bridges had beaten the RIAA, winning a decision in his client's favor.

Bridges attacked by filing for summary judgment. Hollywood responded by modifying its position: We're okay with filters, as long as the movie studios, not ClearPlay and its competitors, have total control over defining and setting the filters. This brews even more controversy as the court tiptoes into the delicate subject of defining levels of pornography, vulgarity, and ethnic slurs. Even the Supreme Court has had a hard time trying to define pornography; about all anyone seems able to agree on is that pornography is hard to define, but you know it when you see it. The legal issue became so much in the public eye that Intel's attorneys filed an amicus brief (an offering from a person or entity not directly involved in the case, prepared at its own cost) that supported ClearPlay's legal argument. Intel had one of the most prestigious legal teams in America, and for them to come out of nowhere and support the legal position of this tiny start-up added to its clout.

Leveraging Controversy and Pushing Buttons

Playing from the same deck as Howard Stern, ClearPlay aimed to leverage the controversy to the hilt. When Howard Stern leveraged to his advantage the media stories about his fines, his audience rose by 22 percent. Going after a similar goal, ClearPlay refined its message, pushed people's buttons, and took full advantage of the media coverage.

The sound bite read and heard across America became that of constitutional rights. Namely, "Who controls the remote control in your house—you, or Hollywood producers?" A reporter's subtext to this might discuss the constitutional right a citizen has to choose whether he preferred to watch a movie the way Hollywood had made it, with the swearing and violence and nudity intact, or preferred to watch it sanitized up to fourteen different ways, with the holder of the remote being the ultimate decider.

Howard Stern uses the same argument quite effectively. If you don't like my content, fine, it's not for everyone. Just change the channel with a push of a button. In fact, Stern's people contacted ClearPlay several times to discuss ways of working together.

ClearPlay launched a Howard Stern–type campaign, which went something like this:

> With a push of a button, you decide what to watch in your own home.
> If you give that right to a handful of Hollywood movie directors, you're letting them hold the remote control.

The approach proved especially effective with the media because it flirted with the *C* word—censorship. Most often, censorship is viewed as Big Brother preventing us from reading certain books and seeing certain movies.

But with the Dixie Chicks, the bigger media story was about

how people were retaliating against the entertainment industry, after one of the Chicks remarked from the stage during a London appearance that she was ashamed that the president—George Bush the second—was from Texas. Radio stations responded to public outcry against the group and censored them in reverse—taking them off the air.

Start messing with constitutional rights and Americans get ornery. And ClearPlay capitalized on this. They started pointing the finger at guys driving $200,000 cars as the ones trying to take away your constitutional rights. Make a claim like that and the media starts writing! ClearPlay hired a PR firm to push this message and the press paid attention. As the PR firm leveraged this message again and again, it gained ink in the *Wall Street Journal, Forbes, USA Today,* and *Time,* and rode the airwaves of four hundred TV reports in outlets like Fox News, plus Jay Leno's monologue on *The Tonight Show.* The David-and-Goliath story never gets old.

Pushing Even More Buttons

When people lie (especially those in the public spotlight), people take notice. We don't need to remind Bill Clinton of this. But just lay out the facts for the media and they relish the story; sometimes they even run with it—going out on their own to dig and write follow-ups. So what was button number 2 for ClearPlay? A story that illustrated how Hollywood directors were speaking out of both sides of their mouths; it went something like this:

Why are Hollywood directors so concerned about ClearPlay? They say they don't want to compromise the "artistic integrity" of their works. Yet everyone knows that if a movie does well, you'll see it on TV in two years. In movies edited for TV, the "S" word is replaced with "sugar" or "shoot" and nudity is screened out. Made-for-TV versions of movies are as common as cows in Kansas. So how can someone like Spielberg say he doesn't want to screen out swear words when he knows full well that the TV networks screen out his "artistic integrity"? Because he makes money from the network, and he doesn't make money from ClearPlay. It's not about "artistic integrity," it's about the money!!

Without exactly calling them liars, lay out all the facts for the press, and it's a juicy story. Rich guys wanting to get richer. Why are they so afraid of an eleven-person company called ClearPlay? Isn't it great to see some of the wealthiest Hollywood honchos get their shorts bunched up because of a spunky, smart start-up? Roger Ebert described the amount of dirt ClearPlay has kicked up by calling CEO Bill Aho "the most hated man in Hollywood." Love it or not, Aho finds himself being called new titles on the Internet (such as Chief Whore), which only adds more controversy to both sides of the story and more prime media fodder.

Now and Beyond

Fast forward to ClearPlay's launch: May 2004. ClearPlay CEO Bill Aho testified for Congress, getting even more press coverage. It's not just by luck, either. ClearPlay hired the Dutko Group, a lobbying firm in Washington, D.C., and proactively created more buzz and controversy, getting senators and congressmen talking about constitutional rights. HR 4586, introduced in June 2004, was essentially a congressional bill that would exempt ClearPlay's technology of filtering for private home viewing from any claims of copyright violation. The Copyright Office testified that ClearPlay did not violate any copyright laws and the Consumer Electronics Association issued a press release supporting the bill, which, as of this writing, is making its way through Congress.

All of ClearPlay's competitors have zero media exposure. Meanwhile ClearPlay, after staying the course with a PR firm, lobbying firm, and buzz strategy, became synonymous with the entire industry of entertainment-content filtering. The likes of Time Warner,

Comcast, Cablevision, and DirecTV now recognize ClearPlay as the industry leader, and are in discussions with them on deals that neither party will discuss publicly.

When Intel filed its amicus, it began paving the way with credibility. With RCA as the manufacturing partner this time, Wal-Mart began selling the first ClearPlay–enabled DVD players in 2004 (several years after Sanyo got cold feet), and continues carrying the product line. Industry experts anticipate that by 2008, ClearPlay will be standard in more than 50 percent of home DVD players produced.

When Janet Jackson slipped the nip to fifty-one million Super Bowl households, American parents, both prudes and nonprudes, launched a firestorm, annoyed that their children had seen a public display of a private part. The seven-second delay became the norm, and content filtering shot up in popularity.

Legal battles continue with Hollywood, while Congressman Lamar Smith, chairman of the House Judiciary Subcommittee on Courts, the Internet, and Intellectual Property, strongly pushes Hollywood and ClearPlay to resolve their legal suits. He has intimated that Congress will pass its own legislation if Hollywood can't play ball with ClearPlay. Although Hollywood's directors continue to dig in under the banner of "artistic copyright infringement," the eight Hollywood studios seem to be warming to ClearPlay and might even decide to partner with the company. (It may help that Wal-Mart is the largest seller of movie DVDs. ClearPlay is also in discussions with several cable networks as well as cable providers.)

The future for ClearPlay? Most likely Video On Demand—movies you can call up and watch on your cable system or satellite system anytime you want. Eight million households subscribe to On Demand services; by 2010, On Demand could be as popular as HBO, in perhaps as many as 30 million households. ClearPlay is looking at a scenario in which customers might see it easily worthwhile to pay $2 or $3 a month for the ability to filter the programming, selecting their own preference for type and degree of explicitness with the touch of a button. Add all this up—$3 a month times 12 months times 30 million households—and you could be looking at a company going from an idea to doing $1 billion a year in revenues. For the company and for people who live by what we've come to refer to as family values, the future looks rosy.

Recap

What about all those investors who swore up and down that "real marketing" works?

By and large, they're following the same herd as all of ClearPlay's competitors—right where they started, and hardly anywhere to be found.

Imagine proposing to operate a business with a marketing budget comprised almost entirely of legal, PR, lobbying fees, and pushing buttons. One hundred percent devoted to capturing media attention but completely ad-less—and with no familiar marketing. You'd be laughed at. Buzzmarketing is a practice. When done well, buzz works.

CHAPTER TEN

The Third Secret—
Advertise for Attention

Once upon a time, there were three little networks. TV clickers didn't exist, and door-to-door salesmen were actually given the courtesy of the time of day. From a marketer's perspective, things were great. People paid attention to you, and you had few ads competing for consumer attention.

The Way It Is

That was the way it was. Today, as you very well know, TV remote controls are a must. Viewers zap more than 63 percent of TV ads. The average cable watcher can choose from more than a hundred channels. Some 25 percent of all TV time is ad related. Most TV shows get one-tenth the ratings that they did thirty years ago. Marketers are launching new products and extensions of their product lines left and right (as just one example, over 166,000 book titles will be launched this year). People are sleeping less, working more, and feeling inundated with the more than a thousand ad messages each of us is bombarded with every day.

Hello, marketers—are you listening? The truth is, your ads aren't having much impact.

Proof? According to a study by the American Academy of Advertising, when a TV commercial comes on, 92 percent of us change the channel, mute the commercial, ignore the commercial, or divert our attention to something else. Don't forget TiVo, either; 71 percent of people interested in TiVo said the feature they liked the most was the ability to skip the commercials.

One of the most comprehensive advertising studies of the magazine sections in Sunday newspapers performed in the 1970s showed what you might expect: One's ability to recall advertising relates to the thickness of the magazine. The *more* advertising in a given medium, the *less effective* each advertisement.

More clutter, less impact.

Bad news for those in the United States, because it's the most cluttered ad market in the world. America spends more on advertising than Mexico's entire gross domestic product (something over $230 billion each year).

How do you measure clutter? On a macro level, it's easy. In the following graph, you'll see what I call the Clutter Curve—an index of

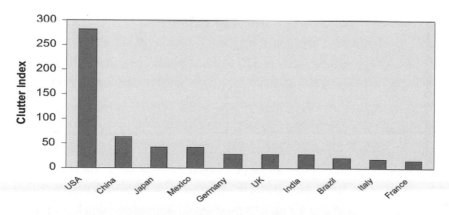

Clutter Curve; lower numbers indicate less ad clutter.
(SOURCE: WARC 2003 AD SPEND; MCCANN-ERICKSON U.S. AD SPEND; ITU—TV SETS PER 1,000 PEOPLE; AD SPEND IN MILLIONS)

total ad spend as a ratio to total TV sets. It shows the U.S. ad clutter, with a 283 Index. China ranks second, Japan third, Mexico fourth.

The less ad clutter in a country, the more likely an advertiser's message will break through.

An average night of prime-time TV presents to the American viewer approximately 128 commercials and promotional messages. One TV commercial would command $\frac{1}{128}$ share of mind (presuming the viewer was paying full attention to all the commercials). Take that $\frac{1}{128}$ of mind share and multiply it by the 8 percent of us paying full attention to TV advertising—and what you get is not a pretty picture.

For the Math Obsessed

Clutter-free media is not your conventional media. But the economics are simple: Your one TV ad competing with 128 other ads in a night provides you a statistical chance of breaking through the clutter of 1 in 128, or 0.8 percent. Now index this 0.8 percent against the 8 percent of us who give TV ads our full attention, and you've reached $\frac{6}{100}$ of the people Nielsen tells you you're reaching. Nielsen provides audience statistics for programming, not for commercials.

But Nielsen says you're reaching 5 million people with that one ad, and you pay the network $10 to reach every 1,000 people (the ad costs you $50,000). Multiply $\frac{6}{100}$ by 5 million, and divide by the $50,000 you paid for that commercial. You effectively reached 3,125 people at a cost of $16 per person.

Hell, at $16 per person, it would be cheaper for you to pay people $10 to stop what they're doing and devote their full attention to watching your ad for thirty seconds. Ten bucks per viewing—much cheaper! Do you understand the difference between impressions and connections now? Pay attention to the economics.

Media expert Ken Sacharin said it best: "Our 'rules' [of advertising] are rooted in another time—a time not too long ago when it was far safer to assume that we already had people's attention and that all we had to do was inform, persuade, educate, and sell."

The smart folks are catching on. If you assume you have people's attention, you are dead wrong. Rule number 1: Get their freakin' attention. Don't follow the herd, because you won't get heard.

Merrill Lynch's media and advertising industry analyst Lauren Rich Fine has pointed out the challenge. "Advertisers have many new choices as well as a yen for more measurement of results," she has said.

Remember the question about a tree falling in the forest and nobody hearing it? If an advertisement is placed and nobody notices it, was the brand ever advertised?

So what should you do? Here's a place to begin:

Maxim 1: Balance Your Media Diet to Maximize Attention

You can achieve much greater impact by bringing balance to your media diet—the types of media you're using for advertising. A balanced diet will recoup a much greater impact. In other words, diversify. Investors do it. Advertisers need to do it, too.

The respected research firm of Millward Brown analyzed brands putting a disproportionate amount of their budget—80 to 90 percent—into TV alone, versus brands putting less of their budget into TV—under 50 percent. They found that the brands with balanced media diets—50 percent or less going into TV—achieved higher awareness levels for their money. In fact, the brands with a balanced media diet spent 76 percent less on advertising to achieve the same dollar per awareness point.

Balance your media diet, and you could get 76 percent more bang for your buck.

Leading advertising media expert Erwin Ephron objectively analyzes media expenditures through complicated optimization models. Those models reveal that sinking disproportionate amounts of money into traditional media produces a diminishing return on investment. So how can you optimize your media expenditures? Spend your advertising dollars in a wider variety of media and you'll produce a greater response for the same ad dollar. Move money out of television, and you will see a far better return on your ad dollar.

TV Time

TV definitely has its role in an advertiser's media mix, but even ad agency executives recognize that "the 30 second commercial is becoming obsolete." In fact, Erwin Ephron indicates that advertisers are gradually breaking their habit from heavy TV dependency. "It's not rampant," he explains, "but it's inevitable."

TV is probably the biggest source of advertising waste—for a number of reasons. In order for TV ads to succeed, they must truly be outstanding—and the odds of producing outstanding TV ads are slim.

Don't get me wrong, TV can be a great medium. It can seize your eyes and ears, and it can make you laugh, buy, and perhaps even cry. If used intelligently with creative ads that look like no other, it can work. I even recommend it for some of my own clients launching new products.

But every year, advertisers continue to pay more and more for TV, while Americans pay less and less attention to it. Not to be too melodramatic, but I compare TV advertising to crack. It will get you high when you first start using it but the more you use, the more it takes to deliver the exact same results. TV is an expensive crack habit.

There's still one more twist of fate in TV. Brian Steinberg, the *Wall Street Journal*'s advertising correspondent, gets to the heart of it:

> *TV advertising is one of Madison Avenue's high profit margin products, so ad agencies are loath to stop selling it. . . . Rather*

than being the sum of an ad campaign, TV spots quickly are be-
coming just one part of the puzzle. . . .

Take a more balanced approach. Diversify your portfolio of ad dollars. Balance your media diet. The benefits of diversifying are no longer in doubt.

Maxim 2: Use Clutter-Free Media to Capture Attention

There's no question that traditional media (TV, print, and radio) may play a role in your marketing mix. But you need to pursue what I call clutter-free media—meaning media that doesn't compete with any other advertising, media that captures 100 percent mind share. The economics of clutter-free media are far more favorable. With clutter-free media, you won't get lost in the clutter— you can reap 100 percent mind share.

I know—you're probably thinking it's not possible to find clutter-free media in today's cluttered world. Who wouldn't want to be a medium's only advertiser? It's what we'd all love to have. But in the real world, we know that sort of opportunity just doesn't exist.

Not so, my friends. Not so. It *does* exist.

EXAMPLE 1—BURMA SHAVE

In 1925, Burma Shave was a small business trying to grow just like any other company. The owners, the Odell family, tried marketing their brand with radio and print. But conventional media failed them—they weren't giving the brand any attention. Forced to consider other alternatives, young Allan Odell decided to create an entirely new, clutter-free medium. He tried to convince his father to place roadside signs along Midwest highways advertising the product. His father said no. But Allan persisted, and his father finally allowed the idea, putting $200 behind it.

At the time, modern-day billboards did not exist. Odell and his brother placed a series of sequential signs along highways, each displaying a partial piece of the advertisement. Eventually, Odell discovered that a slight sense of humor and rhyme caught the attention of travelers—a little easier in those days, when the design of cars and the condition of roads resulted in speeds well below today's. But most important, the absence of any other billboards meant there were no other ads to compete for a car passenger's attention. Odell was taking advantage of undivided mind share.

Each sign in a group had very few words, good for reading as the car swept past. One series of six signs read:

> Said Juliet
> To Romeo
> If you
> Won't shave
> Go homeo
> —Burma Shave

The signs spread all across the nation, becoming an American landmark in advertising and garnering enormous coverage. Radio and newspaper writers loved to do pieces about the campaign, like the series of signs that offered a free trip to Mars to anyone who sent in nine hundred jars of Burma Shave; a supermarket manager called the company's bluff with a collection of nine hundred empty Burma Shave jars . . . and received his free trip to Mars (Moers, Germany, that is—"Moers" is pronounced "Mars").

Every business needs to evaluate its advertising similar to Burma Shave. If conventional means don't work (expect it: The odds are against you), then screw convention. Find another avenue—a clutter-free avenue where you can take advantage of 100 percent mind share.

Example 2—A Bit Nutty . . . But So Was Burma Shave

I faced a challenging situation in the second year of Half.com. In the first year, getting the town of Halfway to change its name got us tremendous press, and selling the company to eBay kept us in the news. But as with any business, continuing growth is a constant challenge. In subsequent years, how do you keep your brand fresh? How do you keep people talking about your brand even more?

Every marketing dollar we spent had to get a strict return on investment. We knew from experience in our first year that the economics of conventional media like TV and print didn't hold water for us. No way were we going to match the spending of an Amazon.com or an eBay, so we had to out-think our competition instead of out-spend them.

Like Burma Shave, we needed to create entirely new, clutter-free media instead of competing in crowded conventional media. Even if we could find a magazine or broadcast spot where we were competing with only two or three other ads, those two or three decrease attention exponentially. Focused mind share was what we were after—no other ads competing in our environment.

Like Burma Shave, we used clutter-free media.

One of our first experiences in the clutter-free approach came right out the blue. Like most marketing vice presidents, I got a lot of calls soliciting sponsorships, and traditional media. One day I got a call from a guy selling advertising space on peanut bags used by street vendors in New York City. I liked the idea. It was clutter-free and it was different.

We put an attractive offer on the peanut bag using a humorous edge like Burma Shave's: "Why pay more when you can get 'em for peanuts . . ." We would later use different headlines like, "You'll go nuts over our prices." Corny, yes. But we had a self-deprecating sense of humor, which got people talking about us, and it was clutter-free media that didn't compete with forty other peanut bag ads. We were it! We had 100 percent mind share.

We measured impact in two ways. First, by word of mouth itself. How many times do people come up to you and say, "Hey I saw your ad in a magazine the other day." Hardly ever. But even two hours from New York City, numerous people came up to me and remarked on our peanut-bag advertising. Second, we measured impact through what I call MIRP (Media Impressions Beyond Rating Points). You can view a full white paper at www .buzzmarketing.com/mirp.html, but it's essentially a formula, calculating equivalent news media value gained, divided by the actual out-of-pocket cost.

We were a brand that pursued the alternative, and it just so happened that this particular clutter-free media fell into our lap. Sometimes we got lucky, but you've got to have your radar on at all times to find clutter-free media.

Example 3—Potty Mouth

This next form of clutter-free media we created defies convention and was one of our most successful and inexpensive ideas. In fact, I still have a hard time believing the long-lasting buzz it created.

Incredibly, this one idea cost $1.34 per unit, a total of $500. It got written up in publications from the *Wall Street Journal* to *Fortune* magazine, landed on *60 Minutes,* and won an Icon Award in the national advertising community. In some circles, it's still controversial, but everyone remembers it.

Here's how it evolved.

Our first offices were in a building where we had a hellacious restroom down the hall. It almost invited graffiti, and that invitation was occasionally accepted. One day I noticed that over the men's urinal, someone had put up a Half.com sticker. I was amused, and I was also inspired that other people in our company—not just me, one of the few people with "marketing" in his title—were branding almost anything to get people's attention.

The sticker remained a few days and then disappeared, probably removed by the janitorial service. It unnerved me a bit. I had grown attached to the fact that every man on the fourth floor was captive to our message. At least in the urinal, we had 100 percent mind share. Undivided attention. Then the sticker was gone, but it had started me thinking. How could we advertise in such a way that the message wouldn't get removed, while still holding onto our captive audience in the context of full mind share?

I decided to see if we could print a message on a urinal screen—the rubberized screen preventing bubble gum, cigarette butts, and other stuff from clogging up the pipes. Sure enough, it could be done. But what would we print? A simple logo seemed very NASCAResque—a mindless logo slapped on without any vivid connection to our brand or context. Once again I wanted Burma Shave contextual humor to make people smile. I also knew we had to push the envelope in order to generate word of mouth.

Ultimately we printed this on the urinal screens: "Don't piss away half your money, head to Half.com." A bit controversial, yes. And we weren't oblivious to the potential risk. In fact, we asked both males and females for their opinion of the copy (not that females would ever see it, but they would certainly hear about it). We knew it would eventually get press, so we wanted to make sure we had the gumption to take the heat and handle it with a sense of humor. It was a go, and we launched the campaign in urinals across Manhattan.

We braced ourselves for the reaction. One of our customer service reps walked into my office and said, "Uh, we got an e-mail about the urinal screen." I thought, "Oh boy, here it comes." Then the rep said, "They want to know if we could send them one."

It caught me off guard. I thought about it, and said, "Sure, why not!" As more time passed, friends and family members called us laughing from their cell phones leaving us messages to the effect, "You'll never guess what I just saw!" Everyone called. Everyone e-mailed. Most were amazed, and most congratulated us for "boldly going where no brand had gone before." And it didn't stop there.

Like it or not, one of the things people talk about is bathroom humor. We got e-mails from semipro baseball teams requesting them for their stadiums. We got e-mails from university professors requesting them for their lectures. We occasionally also got complaints, but the polarity created controversy (which in turn generates more word of mouth). For the most part, though, people enjoyed the laugh, and the urinal screens have now become a strange collectible with friends, family, and customers.

And did we get press! The *Wall Street Journal, Fortune, 60 Minutes.* We got people talking and we got the media writing—the very definition of buzzmarketing.

I couldn't help but compare the success of our urinal campaign to my time in that large corporation when I spent $5 million on automotive racing sponsorships. When we looked at results, we saw zero impact on sales. Zilch. Zippo. Nothing. We were simply another corporate sponsor trying to scream louder for attention, trying to get noticed in a crowded pond. We got no buzz.

This time, though, I got more bang out of a single idea and $500 than from the $5 million spent on racing. By creating our own clutter-free media, we got 100 percent attention, we created buzz, and the press amplified the buzz even more by writing about our innovative, bold marketing.

Out-spend or out-think? You decide.

EXAMPLE 4—YOU WILL LIVE A LONG (AND CLUTTER-FREE) LIFE

When that same little start-up company issued the "same-old/same old" standard press releases, the media paid no attention. They couldn't care less about version 2.0 or our self-important strategic alliances—more boring than a baloney sandwich. What the press loved, however, were our slightly crazy, yet clever, marketing innovations using clutter-free media. It captured their attention as well as everybody else's. As the press covered more and more of our buzzmarketing, we did less and less of the industry standard. We began to rely on what actually got ink—buzzmarketing and lots of clutter-free media.

But how do you get more? We wanted a wide reach—as much reach as *Time* magazine. And finding clutter-free media isn't always as easy as peanuts and urinals. But I was continually on the search. My ideas for new, clutter-free media kept flowing, much to my wife's dismay. In fact, her annoyance continued to grow. Until one day . . .

Being from PepsiCo, I had been thinking about the wide reach of soft drinks and the possibility of using clutter-free media, like soda bottle tops. It didn't feel quite right, though. Would we really get attention on a bottle top? When someone buys a soda, they're thirsty, and they typically rip off the top to get to that cool, refreshing drink. There was maybe a half second of exposure, and the odds of capturing attention in half a second were slim. The key to clutter-free media is length of attention, and focus. So I changed my focus, and came up with the idea that stopped my wife's annoyance. Fortune cookies.

How many people don't read what it says on the little paper inside the fortune cookie at a Chinese restaurant? Not many. Just about everyone reads them—96 percent, according to one study. So what if, in place of the lucky numbers on the back of the fortune-cookie paper, we put an ad for our company? Perhaps the modern-day equivalent of Allan Odell's billboard—the smallest billboard on earth with undivided mind share.

After a lot of research and a little luck, I was talking with the largest single fortune-cookie manufacturer in the country. We struck a deal to be on the back of a projected seven million fortune cookies per week. At that level, we would reach more people than *Time* magazine.

Days after we started running the fortune-cookie ads, the Associated Press picked up the story and newspapers all over America printed it. I was working with the famous marketing guru Joe Sugarman, and as he sat in Maui, he told me CNN had just run a piece on it; so did ABC's *The View,* ABC Radio, and a multitude of publications . . . mostly praising the idea's innovation, while some were critical of its advertising audacity.

While the research says that 96 percent of all fortune-cookie messages get read, we're also told that 67 percent of them get read aloud. I had created my own clutter-free media, broken through consumer attention barriers, and created stories that the press was glad to pick up and carry widely.

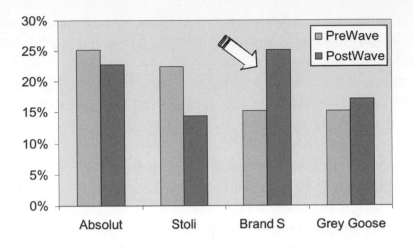

After being advertised in fortune cookies, Brand S vodka
ranked highest in "first comes to mind."

More recently I've turned that idea into a business with the exclusive rights to the world's "tiniest billboards," reaching 32 million people a month. You might even have discovered this book
through one of those 32 million billboards.

As it turns out, fortune-cookie advertising isn't just good for
creating buzz; it also proved to be an effective advertising medium
because of that competition-free, focused mind share. In a survey
conducted with Wharton Business School students for a leading
vodka brand, share of mind increased by 39 percent using fortune-
cookie ads. Before you can capture market share, you need to capture mind share.

Example 5—Hands-On Marketing vs. Sponsorships

One of the typical elements in the marketing mix is sponsorships. If used extremely wisely, they can be effective. But as with
most things, it really depends on your plan. What's the goal, what's
the purpose, and how do you envision it working for you? These
are the critical questions you need to ask yourself before jumping

into sponsorships. Know your market, know your customer, know your costs, think creatively, and understand how you plan to use the sponsorship.

Nevertheless, I fully admit that by the time I arrived at Half.com, the $5 million I had wasted on automotive racing had soured me on the idea. Periodically, people throughout Half.com suggested marketing ideas—some great, and some not so great. One day someone approached me about sponsoring a concert tour. Since we were a marketplace for CDs, there was at least a category fit.

I thought to myself, *What a waste of money.* But whenever I say no to an idea, I try to provide some rationale. I retold the $5 million story. I also recounted another experience from my automotive days. One of the prime consumer groups for automotive accessories and performance parts at Pep Boys was the import drag racing crowd. Kids aged sixteen to twenty-five would tune, lower, and customize their Hondas, Acuras, and VWs. And they would flock to drag strips for regional events where anyone could enter. These were true grass-roots automotive enthusiasts.

A sponsorship at a drag strip might cost $100,000 depending on the size of the local population. But with all the other sponsors at the track, would anyone really remember a billboard with our logo? Would they talk among themselves and say, "Hey, did you see that sponsored billboard at the track?" Not quite.

So what did we do instead of sponsoring a track and wasting our money? We printed up psychedelic purple, oval-shaped bumper stickers with a nostalgic version of our Pep Boys logo (mirrored after the oval, foreign-country stickers labeled, for example, GB). We put these under the windshield wipers of four thousand cars parked outside the speedway. It proved to be clutter-free media, with a targeted demo. And since the sticker design was pretty cool, there was a chance that people would stick them to something permanent and give us additional exposure. Admittedly, it might not generate a tremendous amount of buzz, but it was a heck of a lot cheaper and a lot more effective than a drag strip sponsorship. Ask yourself how many people walk away from a race talking about a billboard sponsor.

So after this detailed diatribe to the eager marketer suggesting the concert tour sponsorship, I said, "Rather than sponsor a concert tour and have a one-dimensional banner hanging on the side of the stage, I'd rather advertise on something that connects with people, like the wristbands for admission to college music festivals." We both stopped and looked at each other.

A little while later, we struck a deal with the largest event wristband manufacturer in the country. Every wristband is clutter-free and every person has that band on their wrist for hours. And more often than not, they wear that wristband home. Again, the key to clutter-free media is length of attention and undivided focus; those are what give you mind share.

To build a brand through conventional advertising channels, most experts will tell you it takes years. Maybe sixty months and $60 million dollars. Most businesses and new brands simply don't have that kind of time, or that kind of money.

In order to capture attention, you've got to break some conventions. You may not need to invest 100 percent of your media dollars in clutter-free media but at least diversify your media portfolio like a financial portfolio—10 percent going into higher risk opportunities. If you've got less to lose, perhaps 25 percent or more. If you place an advertisement and nobody notices it, how much money did you waste?

Maxim 3: Take Off the Shine

Imagine a $7 marketing budget. To BuddyGopher, it was all they needed.

First of all, what's a BuddyGopher? It's the brain child of Nick Gray, who as part of his Senior project at North Carolina's Wake Forest University developed a quirky little service. Developed with software coder extraordinaire Ryan Farley, the program allows people to customize their AOL Instant Messenger "away mes-sages."

The quirky service allows people (the market is mostly high school and college students) to post a message in their profile for their friends to see. Most messages indicate "sleeping," "eating," favorite song lyrics, or links to unusual or humorous images. If you have fifteen buddies, the service allows you to view all your buddies' away messages at once, reducing the total number of clicks from forty-five down to three. To a certain extent, these away messages act as a bite-size blog.

What did a $7 marketing budget get Nick Gray? A whole lot. In four months, he had to stop accepting new users because he had maxed out his server capacity. Seven dollars and four months got BuddyGopher 13,000 users, 150,000 registered screen names, and nine million posted away messages each month and growing. Assuming he translated that into Internet advertising appearing on each away message (they haven't just yet) that would translate into revenue of $250,000 a year. Not bad for two kids and some servers.

But how did they do it on $7?

Nick Gray had some experience doing it the wrong way and the right way. The wrong way? It's another Pepsi story; they usually get it right, but not this time. They were launching AMP, a high-energy drink to compete with Red Bull, and Nick had been hired through an agency to become the AMP ambassador. Pepsi's AMP marketers ran the numbers and decided each college would get two thousand cans of AMP every month. Nick was the key man to distribute these cans.

But do the math: Wake Forest has only four thousand students. Nick and two other people would have to reach 50 percent of an entire school. In order to make the numbers, they had to give out the stuff in cases, not in singles. Furthermore, Pepsi gave a cooler big enough to cool only fifty cans. And warm AMP tasted awful.

The plan and execution from professional marketers stunk. Nick Gray saw that they planted a traditional model on him: Send messages out—job done. But twenty-something Nick Gray knew a lot more than what the marketers saw sitting in front of a spreadsheet. Many more professional marketers would pay substantial sums to have posters put up on prime bulletin boards. That plan might have looked great on a spreadsheet, but walk out into the real world where Miss Minolta, Mr. Motorola, and all their brethren converge, and it's a different story.

The clutter of the posters on campus was overwhelming. All the stuff looked the same, and all the clutter made it hard to stand out. But companies kept pouring money down the clutter crapper, doing the same old thing and thinking their programs were working. Nick Gray knew better—and when it came time to market his own venture, he didn't need a college degree to figure it out.

So in Nick's senior year, as one of his academic requirements, he developed BuddyGopher. Like any business venture, building a product is one thing, but marketing it is a whole different ball game. Nick's first plan of action was to avoid the clutter. A typical plan might be to place flyers in mail folders of students. Real life told Nick that wouldn't work—he saw the trash cans stuffed with thousands of pieces, the debris of this conventional approach.

First, he focused on the freshman, going straight to their dorms. But second, even more important, he would make his marketing look like no other. Would it be on orange paper? Would it use an image of a Gopher? Would it be slick and polished? Hell, no. In fact, Nick Gray went to extremes to make his posters look like "absolute shit" on purpose. Using the PhotoShop software program, he designed an almost horrid-looking color poster and had twenty printed for $7; (visit www.buzzmarketing.com/buddy.pdf to see it).

Why? Because every college student would recognize that the poster didn't come from a big advertiser trying to shove a marketing message down his or her throat. He posted them in high-traffic areas of the freshman dorms.

Two days later, half the freshman class had signed up for Buddy-Gopher—five hundred people. Then it spread to Cornell, Villanova,

Virginia Tech, UCLA, and to Japan, Italy, and Germany. BuddyGopher maintained its transparent personality all throughout its incredible growth. No real logo, no professional branding.

A conscious part of BuddyGopher's aura and communications was to deliberately show the warts of the operation. Yes, at first it might have been strung together with bailing wire, duct tape, and some old servers (and great code)—but the beauty in this was the honesty, transparency, and the personality. What they had was something that brands shun—gobs of personality (yes, gobs of it). They were goofy, warty, rough around the edges, and imperfect. Most brands shudder to think of even writing the word "gobs." But look at Ben & Jerry's ice cream in the early years, and you see the same DNA.

What's so beautifully appealing about this approach? Today, more than ever, if we see corporate shine, we immediately become suspicious. MCI, a corporation that robbed its shareholders and its employees, and former WorldCom CEO Bernie Ebbers still claim it was all just a "misunderstanding." Not only do people disbelieve a company's advertising, they disbelieve the entire company!

Take off the polish, show your warts, and consumers are more likely to trust you and believe you. Nick Gray was not even old enough to rent a car, but he knew. You should too.

Gobs, gobs, gobs, gobs, gobs of personality. Don't be afraid. Get some.

Maxim 4: Turn Your Traditional Media Buys into Buzz to Capture Attention

Okay. Let's say you work for an insurance company or some other traditionalist, do-it-the-way-we've-always-done-it company, and your current corporate environment doesn't lend itself to a media plan using intentionally crappy-looking, creative fortune cookies, urinal screens, or peanut bags. How can you capture attention and create buzz?

You can use your existing traditional media venues, but use

them nontraditionally. In other words, turn your media buys into buzz. You've got to approach it with the sole purpose of creating buzz and capturing attention.

A Different Way to Use Media Like TV

Forty percent of the network TV buys are made far in advance. Let's say you're saddled with that media and need to use it or lose it. What do you put inside that TV time?

Before we go here, let's take a step back. A recent study by Insight Express found that most people who use TiVo or a TiVo-like device will actually watch a commercial, but on one condition only: It has to be a commercial they haven't seen before. If they recognize it as an ad they've seen before, they blast into fast-forward immediately. Poof. Your ad is gone. Money down the tube.

Now, because you're a smart marketer reading this book, you know a secret that not many know. Instead of a handful of commercials, produce lots of *different* commercials. Then people may actually watch them.

Think about our earlier example for Miller Lite (way before the days of modern ad clutter). On average, a new commercial would come out every six weeks and people actually looked forward to them. Remember our friend Dell Schanze of Totally Awesome Computers? He produces a new set of radio spots every week. Think about it: Would you want to go to a Web site and read the same old stuff? No. Today, we want fresh content.

Now you're thinking about commercial production costs. On average, a high-quality commercial will cost upwards of $250,000. They cost too much for you to produce them like cupcakes.

I've made spots for $300,000, and I've made spots for less than $5,000 using stock footage, graphics, some clever copy, a compelling call to action, and some editing time. Your agency may say it reflects poorly on your brand. My response: If viewers fast-forward through it or ignore it because they've already seen the ad, what good is it doing you? Make a cheaper commercial, and you will stand out from the rest of your brethren pack. You'll look a bit unpolished (a good thing if done cleverly), but people are more likely to pause and give your ad a glance as soon as they recognize it's something they haven't seen before. Take off the shine and you may find that people notice and trust you more.

Produce ten times the number of commercials for the price of one conventional ad. Put a unique 800-number or a unique Web site on each, and measure response. Repeat, repeat, repeat. And do it . . . today.

PRODUCT PLACEMENT

Product placement is a bit odd these days. In some cases, you can hire a firm or individual to get your product into movies. It's done more and more. When it comes to TV, currently your product will often be thrown in at no charge if you're advertising fairly regularly on a particular show.

The key, however, is to get your product written into the script and become an integral, meaningful part of the show. Recall AT&T Wireless text messaging on *American Idol.* Or the way Absolut became the focus of an entire episode on *Sex and the City.* But you don't want the product just to be seen; if possible, you want to get a verbal mention, which is worth far more than a product shot.

Why? An audio stimulus stays in the brain five times longer than a visual image before it starts to fade. To prove this, I often play a game to demonstrate the power of word of mouth and its superior memory capacity. It's called Name That Tune, and everyone over thirty remembers it. I tell my audience of senior execs that someone in the room will be able to name a tune I present in two notes. Everyone smiles in disbelief, but salivates at the challenge. I then hum the two notes to the theme music of the movie *Jaws.* Inevitably someone in the group gets it right away. I then ask the exec if he or she has recently seen the movie on DVD or rerun. Almost always they say no.

Then I point out something incredible. They've stored the *Jaws* theme song in their brain for twenty years. Twenty years, and they were able to retrieve it from memory just like that. There is power in audio. If you're using traditional media like TV, get aggressive with your networks and cable stations and get yourself a verbal mention. It's powerful.

BREAKING GROUND

What's an example of breaking ground? Brands like Courvoisier getting woven into song lyrics.

And perhaps ideas like this:

A while back, the Fox TV network raised a stink regarding the production costs of its NFL football games. Specifically, it cost the network a million dollars for the technology to superimpose the yellow first-down line. The network yanked the line altogether. But fans had grown attached to the graphic. When yanked, it sparked a huge outcry, drawing the attention of the press.

Musing about clutter-free media opportunities (as I tend to do), I got to thinking. If a company swooped in and branded that yellow first-down line—actually embedded their logo in the yellow line— it would be the branding coup of the year. The advertiser would make Fox whole, and get incredible exposure.

On top of that, and most important, the outrageous marketing act would generate word-of-mouth buzz and cause a stir in the press. Two types of stories would be written. One headline would read, "Brilliant, Audacious Marketing Move." And the other headline would read, "Audacious Marketing Scheme Reeks of Corporate Intrusion." The story in this second article would complain that corporate marketing is taking over our lives, but would certainly acknowledge the white knight effort of giving the fans back their yellow line. The act would spark polarity, building even more controversy and fueling even more word of mouth.

Not for everyone, but one more angle for creating buzz within the constraints of traditional media.

Recap

In general, the reason why advertisers still gravitate to traditional media formats is because they're familiar, routine, and easy. It's also safer to be offering the familiar when presenting a plan to the board of directors or the CEO.

Recognizing that advertisers continue to pay more and more for ads while Americans are paying less and less attention to advertising leads me to say, "Wake up and smell the marketing!"

As the *Wall Street Journal* has written, consumer attention is "the most coveted commodity of all."

Without attention, nothing else happens.

CHAPTER ELEVEN

Building Britney Buzz

So how do you get attention in a crowded world of wannabe entertainers and build a brand like Britney Spears? And what lessons does the Britney experience hold for a marketer like you?

There's one man who knows very well. It's Larry Rudolph—the man who first met Britney Spears when she was thirteen years old, and, along with Britney herself, is undoubtedly behind the buzz of one of the world's most well-known music artists. Larry was kind enough to take the time to share insights on the making of the Britney brand.

Although Britney Spears became a sudden smash hit, the making of the Britney blockbuster brand was far more deliberate. Buzz can happen overnight, but buzzmarketing can't. Buzzmarketing is deliberate, planned, and only successful when combining a grouping of the Six Secrets.

The interesting twist about the making of the Britney blockbuster brand is that the buzz elements she's most renowned for (the snake, the Madonna kiss—and, yes you'll read the inside stories of these in a bit) didn't happen until *later* in her career. The buzz that really launched her focused on two key secrets: understanding the precepts of attention and delivering a great product.

Only later did she begin pushing buttons to morph out of her sugary pop image and sustain momentum into the mainstream.

Attention—The Key to Buzz

In 1995, entertainment attorney and manager Larry Rudolph was contacted by Britney's mother, Lynne, when her daughter was just thirteen. The family entourage came to his office. Mom, Dad, Britney, and even toddler Jamie Lynn.

Painfully shy, Britney could hardly look Rudolph in the eye, and was polite as can be. Yes, sir. No, sir. Thank you, sir. The man who would later take her to worldwide stardom turned her away, but asked her mother to keep in touch periodically.

As her legion of fans know very well, this was no singing-in-the-shower teen who walked in off the street, was instantly recognized as star material, and catapulted to overnight fame. She had spent summers in New York City at the Off-Broadway Dance Center and the Professional Performing Arts School. At age ten, she added off-Broadway actress to her résumé and at eleven became a television performer, singing and dancing for two years as a Mouseketeer on the *Mickey Mouse Club*.

Even with all that experience under her belt, Rudolph knew that a thirteen-year-old solo pop star wasn't going to make it in 1995. Larry understood the very basic element of buzz. You have to be able to get attention—to get undivided mind share. The context of pop music in 1995 wouldn't allow this. Pop music was pretty much out of favor. New Kids On The Block had saturated the market two years earlier, and their audience of eight- to thirteen-year-olds were turning into mid-teens and looking for cooler, edgier sounds. Rap and Rock were in, with Puffy topping the charts. Such is the predictable cycle of pop music: eight- to thirteen-year-olds like sugary pop music because it's melodious, easy to understand, and very approachable. Even parents like it. Then kids grow older and migrate to something edgier. So the market for pop music was self-limiting, each year gaining a new crop of eight-year-olds and losing most of the kids moving out of the age group and onto something else.

Larry Rudolph knew this all too well. In order to succeed, sometimes you need to wait. And he did. Every month Lynne Spears would call. Friendly updates, chitchat, and the burning question, "Is it time?"

Every month for two years, they would have the same conversations. Until June 1997, when the conversation didn't end on the usual keep-in-touch theme. Teen music mogul Lou Pearlman wanted to sign Britney to a girl band called Innosense. Lynne wanted to know what Larry thought—should she sign?

It had been two years since Larry had seen Britney Spears. She was fifteen now, and he wanted to see some recent photos and a tape of her singing. Britney sang into a tape recorder over a Whitney Houston karaoke song, and Lynne sent the tape and some snapshots off to New York.

Larry was eager for the tape to arrive. He knew the market was changing. As he had expected would happen, pop was coming back. Hansen was hot, Spice Girls were hot, Backstreet Boys were hot. Would Britney's career be best served following the crowd—competing with the Spice Girls and more girl bands likely in the making at record labels all over the country? No. Larry Rudolph knew the girl band segment would soon be crowded. But he could see another opportunity: a wide-open market for a white, female, solo pop artist.

The market for attention was perfect. Statistics play a critical role in the first building block of buzz—attention. Fewer competitors mean good things for you. Place yourself in a situation, any situation, where you have fewer rivals competing for attention, and guess what? The fewer competing for attention, the more likely you are to get attention. The situation to grab mind share was ripe. And that's critical for buzz.

Larry Rudolph envisioned it, saw it, knew it. While obvious in hindsight, this critical first step in Britney's success wasn't so obvious to many experts.

For the pitch to the record labels, Britney needed a professional demo. Songwriter Darren Wittington had written a song for Toni Braxton that didn't make it onto the Braxton album. Phone calls were made, and the unused song became available for Britney's demo. The tracks with Braxton's vocals were stripped from the premix, and Britney's vocal tracks would be laid down instead. Britney listened to the original song with Toni's vocals, rehearsed every day for a week, and then went into a studio to record her vocals over the song. No voice coach in the studio, no producer, only one lone sound engineer in the booth.

Toting what may have been one of the least expensive demo tapes ever to lead to a major career, Britney was off to New York on a ticket paid for by Rudolph, since resources were tight for the Spears family. She flew in on the earliest flight, Rudolph escorted her to the four labels for the pitch, and she left on the last flight out that night.

The pitch was simple. Pop music was back, and there was a wide open market for a white female solo artist. Fill that void with someone like Britney Spears, and you can get attention and sell records.

Three of the four labels said no. It wasn't that they didn't like Britney, but they said the pitch was wrong. All three labels said the pop demographic of eight- to thirteen-year-olds wanted bands, bands, bands, and everybody's evidence was Backstreet Boys and Spice Girls. They said there wasn't going to be another Madonna, another Debbie Gibson, or another Tiffany. Just wouldn't happen . . . no way.

They were following the herd.

But Clive Calder, then head of Jive Records, called Rudolph two weeks later and asked to meet. Rudolph had known Clive for years, and both had been wanting to work together for some time.

Clive wasn't totally convinced yet. He told Rudolph something along the lines of, "I've been thinking about this a lot, and I think you're right." But though he could see a wide open market for a white female solo artist, he had reservations. "I'm not so sure if Britney Spears is the right one to fill that void and sell records. She's got a great look. You tell me she can dance, but she sounds too much like Toni Braxton."

Rudolph promptly explained the story of how they secured the demo tape. He went on to underscore her flexibility, insisting she could morph into Clive's vision for a new pop mold.

The fate of Britney Spears's career teetered, awaiting one man's decision.

Clive thought about it, and then agreed to take a measured risk. Instead of a full advance, he would gamble half the agreed upon advance; Britney would go into the recording studio for a month. After a month, if Jive Records didn't like what it heard, they could terminate the contract. Britney Spears would be free to go elsewhere, if there was still an elsewhere for her to try.

He was offering a vote of confidence for Rudolph's vision and a fair shake for then unknown artist Britney Spears.

Delivering a Good Product

The stage was set. Britney Spears and her manager Larry Rudolph were on the line to deliver the goods.

Getting attention is critical to any brand. But get attention and fail to deliver a good product and you're sunk. If it stinks, no one will tell their friends about it, and no reporters will write about it. You don't have buzz if all you get is attention. That's not enough.

Rudolph was determined to deliver a good product and, like most executives, knew the key to delivering a good product would be the people behind it. In this case, some of the key people behind delivering a good Britney product would be producer Eric Foster

White, songwriter Max Martin, and comanager Johnny Wright. But of course the big burden was on the young shoulders of Britney herself.

When she first entered the recording studio for the Jive Records recording sessions, Britney Spears's voice was much deeper than her highly recognizable trademark voice of today. Her delivery sounded much like something from her earlier performances on Ed McMahon's *Star Search*—lower, and less poppy. Eric Foster White changed all that. With Britney's flexible voice, he shaped her voice over the course of a month to where it is today—distinctively, unmistakably Britney.

At the end of the month, a tape was delivered to Jive's Clive. He listened, he liked what he heard, and he was on board for the full run. Britney went back into the studio to record a complete album.

When it was done, it was good but not good enough. The album lacked anything strong enough to become a smash hit. All along, Rudolph had been wrangling for ace music writer Max Martin, in Sweden, to write a song for this all-important debut album. But Max was in a different league than the unknown Britney Spears. You couldn't just call up Max Martin and order a song, not even for an exorbitant sum of money. Max dealt with known stars.

Then they caught a huge break.

At the time, TLC was the hottest band on the market. Clive Davis had asked Max to write a song for TLC, called "Baby One More Time." As it turned out, "Baby One More Time" didn't end up making it into the TLC album. Clive Davis called Max, explained the situation, and said he would use the song for one of his boy bands.

Max Martin was furious. Even though Clive had truly intended to use the song for TLC, it was possible to see how this could appear as if one of the most heralded pop songwriters had been duped into a bait and switch. But a compromise was reached. The song wouldn't go to a boy band; instead it would go to a new hopeful,

Britney Spears. Martin cooled, and Britney was put on a plane to Sweden, where she would record "Baby One More Time" and two other Max Martin songs.

"Baby One More Time" was the exact smash they were looking for. Once it was recorded, everyone knew Britney Spears would get tremendous airplay. And as with any business, having the right players is key to delivering a good product. Without a doubt, "Baby One More Time" put Britney on the map, and was critical to delivering a great product that radio stations would air, kids would sing, and parents would buy. Martin would continue to write more and more pop songs for the Britney team, reaching millions of ears across America and the world.

Unique voice—check. Smash song—check. Exposure . . . enter *NSYNC. The wildly popular new teen band was touring across the nation, and Larry Rudolph made it key to his Britney effort. The first thing he did was score Britney the opening act for *NSYNC on their tour.

Britney had been getting radio airplay before the beginning of the *NSYNC tour, so when she opened up for them, she was moderately known. But once the music video was released halfway through the tour, her popularity zoomed. People were just as excited to see Britney Spears as they were to see *NSYNC. By the end of the tour, her success was worldwide.

The team had delivered, but most of all it was Britney Spears herself who delivered. Make no mistake, there are two Britney Spears: There's the pretty typical twenty-something kid from Louisiana, and then there's Britney Spears the entertainer. When she's on stage or on camera, she's playing a character, entertaining to the hilt.

Perhaps the best illustration of this is the difference between the ABC Diane Sawyer interview and her role hosting NBC's *Saturday Night Live*. With Diane Sawyer, she wasn't "on". . . not trying to entertain, sing, or dance. She was just herself. Perhaps a bit clunky. Perhaps caught in the lair of Sawyer's many years of interview experience. But just the same, no different than your average American kid.

Contrast that with just a few years earlier, hosting and singing on *Saturday Night Live,* and the difference is like night and day. Only eighteen years old when she hosted *SNL,* she came across poised, funny, confident yet humble, and a consummate entertainer. When she's on camera, she's got camera magic. She's got that "it" presence. Executives from Jive Records begged, urged, and pleaded with Spears and Rudolph *not* to have her host the show, wanting her just to sing. They thought she would screw up under the bright lights of a television stage. But what they didn't know was that Spears transforms herself when the lights are on, cameras are rolling, and she hears the word *action.*

I liken the transformation to an experience I had meeting Heidi Klum in person at the Indy 500. I thought to myself, she's attractive, but I definitely wouldn't peg her for a supermodel. But three days later when I looked at a picture of her, she was a different person. On film taken by just an everyday sports photographer, she glowed (and I melted).

Spears has the same effect. When she turns on her character, she delivers a great product with professional instincts like no other. World renowned photographers from Annie Liebovitz to Patrick De Marchelier to Mark Lidell, people who have worked with hundreds of models, say the same thing—they've never worked with anyone as intuitive or as professional as Spears.

Her intuition perhaps saved her from stumbling on the music video of *Baby One More Time* that would be the make-or-break test for her. When she saw the document describing the creative treatment planned for the video, which had her fighting with an animated monster, she simply said, "My audience won't go for this."

According to manager Larry Rudolph, she mapped out what her audience would respond to right off the top of her head: Britney tapping a pencil, waiting for the school bell to ring, and bam, the dancing begins. Lots of good-looking kids. Very simple. No gimmicks.

Spears and Rudolph called Jive president Barry Weiss and changed what was to be a video of her battling with an animated monster (at a cost of $800,000) into the idea she spun in less than five minutes (with a price tag of $250,000). And even on the set, as wardrobe production people tried to dress her for her video, she changed the wardrobe based on her own instincts—sparking the belly button fad that continues to rage. (Sometimes a teen best knows what a teen audience wants).

When the camera is on, she becomes an entertainer capable of delivering truckloads of excitement—enough excitement to sell twenty-two million *Baby One More Time* albums worldwide. Not bad for a debut. Spears rolled off the tour and right into her second album immediately, which turned into a repeat performance.

The record labels that said Larry Rudolph was absolutely wrong, wrong, wrong were listening now. Understanding the fundamentals of attention and building a team to deliver a great product got Britney's team international buzz beyond imagining. But how do you keep momentum going?

By pushing buttons.

Pushing Buttons—The Key to Continued Success

Spears's first two albums were released just over a year apart. With her second album, she proved she could do it again. More pop. More of the same brilliant Britney style.

But album number three would be fundamentally different. The same pop cycle that ushered Britney in could escort her out. Those eight- to thirteen-year-olds who grew up with her would be going off to look for that edgier, "cooler" music.

Her sophomore album withstood the test, and her spotlight was hot as she dated Justin Timberlake, stoking the media fire even more. But in order to stay current, she had to break with her past and get edgier herself.

Most important, she would need a marketing coup. At the time, the traditional record industry was beginning its multiyear slide. In the fourteen- to twenty-one year-old segment, music download sites Kazaa and Morpheus were threatening the status quo.

Awareness wasn't the issue; just about everyone in the world knew Britney Spears. But how many TV ads, print ads, or even billboards could change her entrenched pop image?

What ensued was perhaps the most innovative campaign in recent music marketing: Create a movie to market her third album and reinvent her as a hard-edged, sexier Britney brand. It's sole purpose: a marketing tool.

The idea of putting Britney in a movie had been around for a while. Ann Carli, who had worked for Jive Records' parent, Zomba, had approached Larry Rudolph with the suggestion. At the time, it was simply a generic pitch—let's make a movie with Britney. But as time went by and the people involved faced up to the challenging task of how to reinvent the image of Britney Spears, the idea took on weight. It began to look like just the vehicle to market her third album and reinvent her image.

TV writer Shonda Rhimes was brought in to write the screenplay, but on reading the treatment, Spears said it wouldn't cut the mustard. And just as Spears had reworked her *Baby One More Time* music video off the top of her head, Larry Rudolph says she did the same thing this time. In a matter of minutes, she created what would become the skeleton for the movie *Crossroads*.

The picture carried a production budget of $11 million, amazingly cheap by Hollywood standards. But it did exactly what it was supposed to—reposition Britney in a more grown-up image. Max Martin was brought in to write several songs for the movie, and the songs were also on Britney's third album, most notably "I'm Not a Girl." The $11 million marketing investment yielded a ten-times return on investment for Clive Calder of Jive Records—$57 million worldwide gross at the box office plus several million in DVD sales and millions of albums sold.

By Hollywood standards, many considered the movie a flop, yet most critics actually praised Spears's acting in the film. But considering the movie's purpose, it may be one of the most unknown coups in music marketing to date.

Britney also began pushing buttons to reinvent herself. Just two months before release of her third album, she would perform at MTV's Video Music Awards. Collaborating with director/choreographer Wade Robson, Spears opened the performance inside a cage, with a live tiger, and the staging also wove in the concept of Britney with a snake. Most thought a photo of Britney Spears in a cage with a live tiger would be the prize photo of the evening, seen around the world. But it was Spears, the consummate camera-savvy performer, who knew the prize photo might be of her with the snake—close up, slightly phallic, and striking a chord with millions. Although Spears convinced reporters and millions of viewers that she had a snake fetish, in truth, the snake gave her the heebie-geebies. She knew the value of the publicity and performed with the snake anyway. Whatever it took to push those buttons.

Fast-forward two years later, months before the launch of her fourth album, and Spears would again push buttons like no other at the Video Music Awards. Yes, it's the kiss.

The idea came not from MTV but from Madonna. As they rehearsed, it was always an air kiss, a peck kiss, never anything dramatic. Ask anyone watching rehearsals, and it wasn't a big deal.

But when cameras went live, Spears, the consummate performer, knew ten million eyes were watching, and the world's media was watching as well. Would the headline read "Britney and Christina Tie Tongue with Madonna at VMAs." No. No one even *remembered* that Christina kissed Madonna. When cameras were live and the show was on, Christina didn't push buttons. She didn't give Madonna that long, lesbian-like kiss that shot around the world. Britney would be the one to push buttons in a big way. The kiss was long enough for still photographers to capture, deep enough to spark controversy (was there tongue?), and taboo enough to get men and women talking about it all over the world.

If there was any doubt that the pop star still clung to her sugar-sweet eight-to-thirteen demo, it was fervently eradicated with the Madonna kiss. Without a doubt, she became more grown up, more taboo . . . and more buzzworthy. Deliberately so. The new mistress of buzz had come into her own.

Recap

In late 2004, Elizabeth Arden contracted with Spears for a fragrance under the Arden label called Curious. Before inking any deal, the cosmetics and fragrance maker performs extensive market research on its celebrity endorsers. The research showed that every single demographic group knew Britney Spears: white, African American, Asian, Hispanic, eight-year-olds, and eighty-year-olds. Four months before the fragrance launched, it had $22 million in preorders.

That kind of awareness doesn't happen by chance. And although many may call the Britney story an undeserved success, that success, as we've seen, was designed and quite deliberate. Buzz often appears to come out of nowhere, but buzzmarketing is a product of design and deliberation.

At multiple points, Rudolph and Spears had the opportunity to jump at impulse. Rudolph could have taken her on at thirteen, but waited two years until the market and situation for undivided mind share and attention was ripe. They could have taken the easy way out and signed with the band Innosense, looking for a quick hit. Innosense got no buzz, and went nowhere.

But by taking a very deliberate approach, Britney Spears has sold over fifty-five million records, and has been dubbed by *Forbes* magazine as the "world's most powerful celebrity."

Perhaps Rudolph knows this all too well, as his ReignDeer Entertainment machine continues to crank out buzz by design. His other projects? Producer, along with papa Joe Simpson, of *The Newlyweds,* the MTV reality show with Jessica Simpson and Nick Lachey—transforming another blonde from peripheral celebrity to buzz icon.

Make no mistake, buzzmarketing is by design and deliberate.

Leaving Buzz Basics, Entering Buzz Leadership

Now that you understand the buzz basics—pushing the Six Buttons of Buzz, how to capture media, and advertising for attention—it's time to take buzz to a higher level.

These next three secrets will require more of your commitment, more of your involvement . . . perhaps combined with more risk.

Here come the secrets of leading your brand and leading your company with buzz.

CHAPTER TWELVE

The Fourth Secret— Climb Buzz Everest

What is Buzz Everest?

And why climb it?

Buzz Everest is making buzz history. Buzz Everest represents achieving the pinnacle of buzz—transforming your brand by doing things no one else has been able to do. Reaching the pinnacle means generating hundreds of news stories that start conversations all across the country.

Buzz Everest is achieving what 99 percent of your competitors would never even attempt. Conquering Buzz Everest is a feat that few will ever attempt, much less achieve. Buzz Everest is treacherous—it's easy to fail if you don't plan, if you don't have courage and faith in your own abilities, and if you don't have follow-through.

But if you conquer Buzz Everest, you will experience the greatest feelings of achievement and realize the greatest amount of buzz—beyond your wildest dreams. Best of all, the payoff from Buzz Everest is huge.

Buzz Everest is when Pepsi created the Pepsi Challenge, and spent millions of dollars on research to prove that "more Coke drinkers prefer the taste of Pepsi." Buzz Everest is convincing a town to rename itself and thereby putting your brand on the map of the United States of America. But Buzz Everest is more than just creative thinking outside the box; it happens by increasing the size of the box and reinventing your company or product with a story that, to most people, is unimaginable.

In today's marketing environment, everyone is following a similar path. The traditional path will get only traditional results. And traditional results means performing the same as everyone else—being satisfied with mediocre or average levels.

If mediocre is good enough for you, stop reading right now. But if you want to experience exquisite and breathtaking results, that's what we're going to look at in the next few pages.

There are two reasons to climb and reach the top. First, you'll prove yourself to be smarter and more creative than others in the profession of marketing. This alone will capture consumer and media attention. But the second reason proves to be far more important. The second reason to climb Buzz Everest is because customers will know that what you have done can't be replicated by your competitors. And customers will respond.

In the Pepsi Challenge, Pepsi spent several million dollars in research and endless in-person surveys to justify their claim that Coke drinkers prefer Pepsi. If Coke had tried to replicate the research, by the time they finished, it would have been too late. Climbing Buzz Everest puts you in a unique position that few of your competitors can ever reach.

Buzz Everest Saves a Doomed Brand

The story of Rit dye is a story of how climbing Buzz Everest saved a doomed brand.

Rit dye?

For several years, I've had the good fortune of being the owner of a Bernese mountain dog. Just about every day, I walk my Bernese on the college grounds in the eclectic little town of Swarthmore, Pennsylvania. One day there, I met a fascinating man by the name of Don Price, who has an Alaskan malamute. Through walking our dogs together, we got to know each other.

I was already working on this book; he asked me to tell him some of the principles and after my very quick synopsis, he said, "You know . . . that's exactly the approach I used with Rit dye."

I had never heard of the product.

Don Price then told me one of the most fascinating stories I've ever heard. It turns out that he was the man who made tie-dye what it is today. But he didn't popularize it through TV, radio, or print. He didn't do it through multilevel marketing. In fact, he did it with zero advertising dollars. In my terminology, he did it by climbing Buzz Everest.

It Started Out Dandy

In the early 1960s, Don went to work for Best Foods, a prominent consumer brand company with products like Hellmann's mayonnaise, Entenmann's cookies, Arnold bread, and Thomas' English Muffins.

Don had the good fortune of being hired by this prestigious company as brand manager for a marquis brand—Hellmann's. He was given a coveted corner office in their New York City headquarters, and he was ready to lead Hellmann's mayonnaise to a higher stratosphere. His job at Best Foods started out just dandy.

But he immediately found his new, high-profile position to be disappointing. His superiors told him that they loved him, but Hellmann's was too big a brand to mess up. All the real decision making took place at higher levels—not at his level. "Then what do I do?" he asked. They admitted that he would not be doing very much.

Don was a sharp, bold thinker and quickly proposed the following to his superiors at Best Foods: "Since I'm not going to have much decision-making responsibility because of the importance of the Hellmann's brand, do you have any low-profile brands I could run? You know, brands I can manage on my own? Brands you couldn't care less about if I screw up?"

"Oh, heavens, yes, we've got dozens of those!" he was told. So shortly thereafter, Don Price was put in charge of an odd little brand called Rit dye.

A Brand with No Future

At the time, Rit dye was a powdered product used primarily by older women to color things like drapes and furniture coverings. The dye was sold through supermarkets, craft stores, and chains like Woolworth's. Its market share was abysmal compared to the leading brand, Tintex. Overall, the brand was dying because its rapidly aging consumers were dying and so no longer dyeing; (sorry—couldn't resist).

In summary, Rit dye had all the ingredients of a dead end: declining sales trends and an entrenched competitor with huge market share.

It was a brand with no future.

But it sold for about forty-nine cents back in the 1960s and cost only seven cents to make. It was clear that the only thing Rit dye had going for it was a healthy profit margin.

Don lobbied for advertising dollars to revitalize the Rit dye brand, only to be summarily denied. Management told him, "You can spend all the time you want on Rit dye, but you have zero dollars for advertising!" His easy path was blown up. So Don was faced with only one other choice: He had to climb Buzz Everest.

Maxim 1: Find Your Buzz Everest and Climb It!

Okay. No advertising dollars meant no traditional marketing approach. Management respected Don, so they were willing to let him do whatever he wanted with Rit, as long as it didn't involve advertising expenses. One of his first stops was the research and development office.

It was rare for R & D guys to see someone from marketing so frequently—most of the marketing honchos were out spending company money. Don's angle, though, was to find a new use for Rit dye. Cataloging all the possible uses for dye, one of the researchers found that it was used in Africa and India to decorate and imprint clothing. The process was called tie-dye (but very different from the tie-dye we see today in America). African and Indian tie-dye had very symmetrical, repeated patterns, almost as if done on a printing press. There might be some international opportunities, but Don decided he would bring the tie-dye process to America. If it caught on with a younger audience, maybe increased sales would reflect the youth market.

But how? How could he influence Americans to use this ancient process still widely used in Africa and India? This was in the early 1960s, when news was spreading of a fast-growing hippie movement. Psychedelic colors were becoming the rage, and the hippies might actually be a market segment interested in using psychedelic dyes to tie-dye their individualistic garb. In New York City, Greenwich Village was the area for opinion leaders and influencers of the hippie movement. So Don went to Greenwich Village to get a feeling for whether he might be able to stimulate interest in tie-dye.

He found artists who were willing to experiment with the tie-dye process. They were enthusiastic, but the process was rather messy as multiple colors mixed and leaked. Don went back to the researchers and convinced them to package the dye products in no-mess liquid dispensers that could be squeezed onto fabric. For example, by keeping the colors from running together, a garment could have yellow dye in the center, with purple swirls around it.

Using this new Rit dispenser, artists were able to create the multicolor designs they desired with ease and without mess. So artists, opinion leaders, and influencers took to tie-dyeing almost as if it were a new psychedelic substance. Janis Joplin began wearing tie-dye and was even rumored to wear tie-dye panties—all made using Rit dye in the new container.

Although it was exciting to have the likes of Janis Joplin getting intimate with the Rit dye brand, tie-dye was confined to a small circle of users and wasn't expanding. Trying to figure out how to spread the tie-dye phenomenon, Don Price invited several fashion editors to Greenwich Village. His hope was to show them that tie-dye was catching on in the Village, and have them endorse it in their articles as the next new fashion trend.

The Madison Avenue editors told Don that the tie-dye fad was just a Greenwich Village thing. Although that was where life was shaking free in New York, as far as the editors were concerned, what happened in the Village had no real impact on fashion trends in general.

For Don, Buzz Everest was getting steeper.

The message Don got from these upscale editors was that it took three key elements to spread any trend:

It had to be associated with something big, something newsworthy.
It had to catch on in Middle America.
It had to be the fashion (meaning truly fashionable, not just a fad).

At about this time, Don told me, his Greenwich Village hippies heard about a musical gathering that was to take place in rural Woodstock, New York. They grasped that it was going to be a big event, and probably memorable. Nobody could have foreseen just how big and how memorable.

Two of the well-known artists in Greenwich Village asked Don

if they could tie-dye several hundred T-shirts to give away at Woodstock. They said they would need a dryer to make that many in such
a short amount of time. Don had salted away enough money in his
corporate budget to pay for a dryer and several hundred T-shirts.
And so the project began. Tie-dye T-shirts lined a loft space the size
of a football field, hanging from crisscrossed clotheslines, taking up
every inch of space.

To the droves of people who ended up coming to Woodstock, the
tie-dye T-shirts were eye-catching. The idea caught on—big. Joe
Cocker wore tie-dye at Woodstock. Mama Cass wore tie-dye. Janis
Joplin wore tie-dye. Tie-dye became a symbol of antiestablishmentar-
ianism. It was a visual statement that "I'm young and independent,"
and, most important, it was *your* shirt. No one else could have the
same shirt as you. It was a statement of being an individual. And the
cause of individualism was the biggest thing in America in the 1960s.

Right after Woodstock, sales of Rit dye began to increase, re-
versing the prior trend but not skyrocketing. Don's project had
caught on, but the danger was that Rit dye would be riding the
coattails of a fad that would quickly fizzle out. He had to move tie-
dye into the realm of fashion and figure out how to make it catch
on in Middle America.

So Don pitched a tie-dye fashion line to designers in New York
City. He was rejected by twenty-three designers. But he found one
who saw possibilities, and that one was a biggie: Halston. The top
of Buzz Everest might be in sight.

Halston was a master of buzz himself. He designed hats for many
celebrities, including Jackie Kennedy. But hats were going out of style
in the early sixties, and he was looking for his next fashion statement.
Halston liked the tie-dye concept, liked the line, and took a chance
on it. He sold his tie-dye to the likes of Cher, Catherine Deneuve, and
Ali McGraw. Soon enough, Ali McGraw was featured on the cover of
a major national magazine . . . wearing tie-dye. Shortly afterward,
Halston used the tie-dye motif in many of his department store bou-
tiques, and tie-dye took off as a bona fide fashion.

A big and buzzworthy fad at Woodstock. Then a fashion with Halston. Don's next step would be Middle America.

How much more Middle American can you get than the Girl Scouts? Don took the idea to the Girl Scouts to create a tie-dye merit badge (not your typical marketing path). Sure enough, several months later, there was a Girl Scout tie-dye merit badge. There were also several appearances on shows like *Captain Kangaroo* to capture Middle America.

A Long Way to the Top of Buzz Everest

In essence, tie-dye started as the antithesis of traditional marketing in corporate America (e.g., Hellmann's mayonnaise). Give most brand managers the option of a job as brand manager for Hellmann's mayonnaise or for Rit dye, most would choose the easy path of Hellmann's. It would be a great job: No hard work, don't rock the boat, and you've got it made. Don, however, took the hardest assignment anyone could imagine: a product with dying sales, a huge competitor, and a dying installed base of customers.

He ended up climbing Buzz Everest for Rit. By reviving Rit dye through nontraditional means, he achieved multiples more than if he had been given a huge budget for traditional advertising. Taking the traditional path would have produced traditional results. Don did things brand managers don't ordinarily do. Instead of taking the much easier path, he chose a path that brought him the exhilarating experience of climbing Buzz Everest. And not only did he transform a loser into success by making tie-dye what it is today, but he has made himself one of the heroes of modern-day marketing.

Maxim 2: Take the Risk

In any business, if you want to see a huge difference in results, you've got to take big risks and do things like climbing Buzz Everest. You've got to be realistic when choosing your marketing direction. Traditional marketing is something your competitors can replicate. Traditional marketing will produce average results. Average results don't build careers, average results don't increase market share, and average results don't skyrocket profits. Climb Buzz Everest. It will make all the difference.

Climbing Buzz Everest requires resourcefulness, follow-through, patience, and faith. Buzz Everest is typically pursued in the face of adversity . . . when you've got nothing to lose.

But only rarely do you find companies willing to climb Buzz Everest when things are going fine. You've got to extricate yourself from the traditional path—the easy path. But turning your back on tradition carries extra risk. What if it fails? How will that reflect on you as a manager or a businessman? Yet you can't eliminate risk and have breakaway growth.

A New Attitude Toward Fouls

Most managers want huge results with little risk. It just doesn't work that way. You've got to encourage risk taking without penalty. Americans by nature hate to lose. We're willing to take risks when there's little downside, especially if we can see a huge potential upside. But when things are going fine, we shy away from taking risks. Not a good idea!

In corporate America, too often it's one foul and you're benched. But in the NBA, every player is allowed five fouls per game. Company managers and executives should be establishing a five-foul rule, and making it known to everyone.

Think about how some of the most successful coaches in the NBA view fouls. If LeBron and Kobe end the game with zero fouls, you know they're not playing aggressively. You know they're not playing their best game. If they end the game with four fouls, they've pushed it to the limit . . . and chances are they've scored more points, gotten more rebounds, and gotten more steals. Once in a while, you foul out. That's part of the game. Winners know one thing all too well: You're not going to win every game.

Let your players (employees) get their fouls. Innovations will come faster, sales will be higher, and you'll learn from failures. At Johnson & Johnson, R. W. Johnson Jr. used to say, "Failure is our most important product." Create a "foul-allowed" environment where you can contemplate climbing Buzz Everest . . . and then enjoy the climb.

Remember the traditional path is risk-free, but it will produce average results, average market share, and average profits. Unless you climb Buzz Everest, you may never know what you missed.

CHAPTER THIRTEEN

War of the Colas:
A Story Behind the Story

At one point in the 1970s, Coca-Cola's market share was 37 percent greater than Pepsi's, and Pepsi was looking at a monumental task. Coke was so confident of Pepsi's demise that CEO Roberto Goizueta remarked that by 1990 Pepsi would be an insignificant factor in the soft drink business.

That prediction fired up the Pepsi Challenge—Pepsi's own Buzz Everest, which, from 1975 to 1983, was one of the most memorable marketing campaigns in history.

It caught Coca-Cola by surprise and caused an increased thirst around the world for details of the fiery competition between two major industry competitors. In a mere eight years, the Challenge resulted in Pepsi passing Coke as the leading soda in supermarkets across America. Coke's market share lead over Pepsi narrowed from 37 to 10 percent.

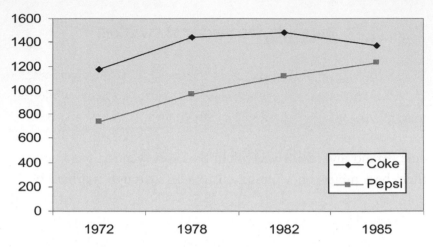

Pepsi and Coca-Cola Sales, Millions of Cases per Year, 1972–1985
(SOURCE: BEVERAGE INDUSTRY ANNUAL MANUAL)

Creating Buzz

So how did a runner-up company like Pepsi manage to become a force that Coke would have to race for first place? It certainly wasn't with flashy commercials because those early Pepsi Challenge ads had no memorable production value and certainly were not visually trendy. In fact, they were judged as bland and boring. But what the Pepsi ads lacked in glitz was made up for in buzz.

Ironically, it was Coke, not Pepsi, that spread the flame by its reaction to Pepsi's challenge. The press simply ate it up (or in this case it might be more fitting to say they drank it up), even naming the intense commercial battle the Cola Wars. Call it media controversy or whatever, but Pepsi capitalized on it big-time.

Necessity, the Mother of Invention

Region by region during the early 1970s, Pepsi's sales were spotty. In some markets, the two companies ran neck and neck, while elsewhere Pepsi was being outsold as much as six to one by Coke.

Pepsi's market share in some of these weak areas was minuscule. Brand awareness was zilch. So Pepsi went to work, putting their best minds on winning customers in tough markets by increasing store promotions, cutting prices, and even doubling advertising. They used conventional ideas based on solidly logical marketing. But still nothing happened. Throwing money at the problem didn't work. The customers still went with Coke.

The Problem with Dallas

One of the most challenging markets was Dallas. At the time, a man well known in the trade named Harry Hersh had recently sold the local bottling plant in Dallas to Pepsi, and had stayed on to work at Pepsi's corporate office. He knew the territory well and used Pepsi's rich resources to prop up the ailing market. Old trucks were replaced, new equipment was added, and Pepsi filled its ranks with energetic employees. Except for marketing, every ingredient possible for success was put into place. The upgrading of people and equipment in Dallas had positioned Pepsi for success, but market share still stunk.

Harry Hersh had seen conventional marketing fail before, and he was convinced that the standard approaches wouldn't work. He pleaded his case to the head of advertising, Alan Pottasch, the only one who would even listen to Harry's dire predictions.

The time was right for Hersh to make a bold proposal. "Give Dallas something different, give Dallas something daring!" Hersh exclaimed. "Our market share is so low, we've got nothing to lose."

Pottasch agreed that, indeed, there was nothing to lose. So the ad agency was charged with resurrecting their Dallas campaign. But what came back from the agency wasn't a campaign that could possibly win customers for Pepsi and didn't make it past the first pitch.

Pepsi's advertising chief reflected on the issue, but couldn't quite put his finger on the problem. He suspected Dallas required an approach only a local agency could provide, so he called a college friend of his, Bob Sanford, who ran a small ad agency in Dallas. Given a clean slate, the Sanford Agency went to work.

Sanford knew the basic issues: Pepsi sales were poor, and brand awareness was even worse. Not being really familiar with much else about the company, the agency launched a series of focus group sessions that included a blind taste test of different cola brands.

Participants in the focus groups were asked to drink several colas and choose the one they preferred. Lo and behold, they picked Pepsi—not just occasionally but about 70 percent of the time. It didn't make sense: People preferred the taste of Pepsi, but they were buying Coke. Most participants were shocked, and some were even angry—feeling they were somehow being tricked. They couldn't believe that their choice was Pepsi. Just as the taste testers were shocked, so was the Sanford Agency.

When the Sanford researchers called Pepsi to tell them what was going on, Pepsi's marketing gurus Norm Sylvester and Pete Reader joined the Sanford team to sit behind a one-way mirror and watch the proceedings. They saw the phenomenon take place again and again. No doubt about it, people were choosing Pepsi.

Sanford copywriter Don Colburn was hit with a burst of inspiration (perhaps not surprising: Don is a Pulitzer Prize–winning writer, for his play *The Gin Game*). He cried out, "I've got it! I've got the campaign: Take the Pepsi Challenge."

This campaign, which would forever change reality for Pepsi (and Coke, for that matter), began as a simple voyeur entertainment for marketing executives, watching focus group participants express preference of one taste over another. Soon, consumers all over the nation would be taking taste tests of their own. And so the Pepsi Challenge was born.

Humble Beginnings

In a vacant storefront at a Dallas shopping mall, the Challenge was set up with a waiting room and a taste-test room. People were asked if they were Coke drinkers. If they were, would they be willing to participate in a taste test?

Five hundred taste tests were filmed, and ultimately about ten were used for TV commercials. Again and again, the taste tests revealed the same conclusion—more Coke drinkers preferred the taste of Pepsi. This was to become the key message in each commercial. But before the TV stations allowed Pepsi to make such a claim on the air, Pepsi would have to prove it.

To comply with station demands for proof, Pepsi commissioned one of the most expensive research projects in its history, using a nationally representative sample. At the Fairmont Hotel in Dallas, the Pepsi people gathered all the data they needed, and introduced the Dallas campaign to the news media. As was to be expected, reporters were suspicious, but Pepsi was quick to assuage any doubts, encouraging the reporters to take the Challenge themselves. They were convinced by their own choices.

The new Pepsi TV commercials for the Dallas market were visually bland, featuring ordinary people in a dreary storefront. But there was one groundbreaking aspect of the commercial that was riveting. At the end of each taste test, Pepsi forthrightly revealed the name of the competing brand; in 1975, this was revolutionary.

Challenging Los Angeles

Since Pepsi had a tiny market share in Dallas (about one-fifth of Coke), the initial buzz generated by the Dallas Challenge commercials wasn't enough to wake up the sleeping Coca-Cola giant just yet. But Pepsi's Los Angeles market manager, Jack Pingel, had high hopes. Pingel suspected that what was starting to work in Dallas would fare just as well in Los Angeles, the second most populated market in the country, and an area where Pepsi was plagued by the same market-share problems.

The process was the same. A vacant storefront rented in a mall where blind tests were taped for commercials. Again the commercials were shown to the news media and again some reporters took the test.

The results were the same, and once more Pepsi made headlines. Consumers took notice. But they weren't the only ones waking up to Pepsi.

Goliath Overreacts

When Pepsi brought its Challenge to Los Angeles, it woke Coke up with a shake. And the company wasn't very happy to be rudely awakened from its peaceful slumber.

Sure, the Pepsi commercials were bland, but they definitely weren't going unnoticed; Coke felt threatened and tried to have the ads pulled off the air altogether, citing that Pepsi's claim (more Coke drinkers prefer the taste of Pepsi) was false. Coke brought its case to the Better Business Bureau's National Advertising Division, the body that decides on disputed advertising claims. Pepsi had its research, and proved the validity of its claims. Coke ad executives fumed. In the end, they couldn't stop the claim because, quite simply, it was true.

Know When to Cut Your Losses

The Coca-Cola Company should have let the matter go, but it-didn't. The buzz generated from the Pepsi TV commercials was a minor brushfire, but Coke's response to them—slick commercials of their own mocking the Pepsi Challenge—was the equivalent of dousing the campaign with gasoline. Instead of ignoring the Challenge ads, Coke ignited Pepsi embers into a full-fledged forest fire.

The first commercial Coke aired criticized the scientific process that Pepsi used in the Challenge. In Pepsi's commercial, two colas were labeled *M* and *Q*. When the consumer said which cola he preferred, it was revealed that *M* was Pepsi and *Q* was Coke.

Coke's critical commercial focused on the letters *M* and *Q*. It started out with a psychologist on camera saying: "You may have seen a recent commercial with a blind taste test of colas. Of course, the commercial is biased and can't be relied upon because of the letters used. As you know, *M* stands for words like mellow and mild. And *Q* stands for queer. It's no wonder that people chose *M* over *Q*."

Pepsi subsequently changed the letters in the filming of the commercial to *L* and *S*. Coke came back with another commercial using the same psychologist. This time, the psychologist attacked the methodology of *L* and *S* because: "*L* stands for lovely, and light . . . and you know what *S* stands for"—a not very subtle reference to the word *sh-t*.

The press picked up on this immediately. The psychologist attacking *M* versus *Q* was one thing, but Coke's continued insistence on the inherently biased nature of letters in the alphabet bordered on ridiculous. Nevertheless, Pepsi took the letters off the cola cups and Coke came back with *more* commercials mocking Pepsi, even inviting consumers to a taste test between Pepsi and Fresca. Coke touted the results, but neglected to mention that more people still preferred Pepsi to Fresca. The press had a field day with Coke's blunders. But the ads and publicity all served a bigger purpose—to fuel the Cola Wars.

Now when Pepsi Challenge commercials came on, people paid close attention. And when Coke's attack commercials aired, people were doubly attentive. The controversy became national news. People wanted to know what all the buzz was about.

In kitchens and living rooms across America, families took their own Pepsi Challenge. People started doing blind taste tests with everything: wine, peanut butter, beer—you name it. The blind taste test joined the ranks of pop culture.

Creating a Pepsi Culture

Thanks to Coke, what had been a buzz for Pepsi morphed into a roar. In Dallas, Pepsi went from 8 percent market share to 20 percent. In the huge market of Los Angeles, Pepsi went from 11 percent market share to 19.

The Challenge impacted every aspect of the Pepsi operation, from its employees to its consumers. It motivated bottlers, and it lit a fire under the guys stacking Pepsi at the supermarkets. Trucks were painted with Pepsi Challenge logos. Salespeople wore Challenge T-shirts as part of their uniforms. Pepsi bottles had bottle hangers encouraging people to try the Challenge at home. More and more Challenge booths were set up outside stadiums, outside shopping malls, and in train stations. Ordinary folks had the opportunity to take the Challenge—just like on TV. Bottlers even begged for the Challenge to come to their markets. From 1975 to 1983, 83 percent of Pepsi bottlers rolled out some form of the Pepsi Challenge. In eight years, approximately 25 million people took the Pepsi Challenge.

Aftermath

The Pepsi Challenge is ultimately a tale of irony. Pepsi's campaign might not have caused more than a small ripple had Coke done, well . . . absolutely nothing. But the number-one company just couldn't help itself; it felt attacked and so it retaliated with an attack of its own (which led to one of the most renowned marketing lessons in history with New Coke).

The difference amounted to 495 billion cases of annual volume for Pepsi, closing its lead from 37 percentage points behind Coke to just 10 points behind.

Recap

In the beginning, Pepsi threw money at the problem. They doubled advertising. Then they threw unconventional smarts at the problem, and climbed their own Buzz Everest. Smarts and guts versus money—these are the building blocks of DNA for buzzmarketing. Out-thinking, not out-spending.

CHAPTER FOURTEEN

The Fifth Secret— Discover Creativity

Who would dare to say that 85 percent of all advertising is invisible? Only an impassioned adman like George Lois (who put MTV and Tommy Hilfiger on the map) would make such a statement. When he's asked his opinion on research-driven advertising, people who know George step out of the way. "Advertising is not a f@#$ percenting science," he roars. "Advertising is an art—no question about it."

Lois theorized that two reasons support his 85 percent observation. First, we've built up immunity to most of advertising's clutter and lack of believability. And second, most advertising proves to be mediocre. And mediocrity equals the kiss of death in advertising.

Roger Enrico, former CEO of PepsiCo, firmly believed that "advertisers get the creative they deserve." If you demand the best, you'll get the best. If you want safe advertising with elevator music and pretty pictures, you'll get what you deserve—ordinary vanilla, not even French vanilla." Unless you demand the best you will become a member, in good standing, of the 85 percent club; you will be comfortably invisible.

When it comes to creativity, Enrico argues that "every individual has immense creative potential. The only difficult aspect is mustering their courage to use it." Enrico says that it is up to leaders to help people find courage by challenging them and encouraging them to dare and dream—"That's the responsibility of every leader."

Whether you're Apple Computer or Al's Computers, whether spending $40 million or $400, advertising dollars should be considered precious. To get the most out of your advertising dollars, you've got to promote and nurture creativity . . . and that takes courage.

After speaking on the subject of buzzmarketing, I'm often asked, "What creative process do you use to come up with the big idea?" I respond honestly, "It's not easy." To get that one gem of an idea, I've had to create and discard seventy more that never see the light of day because, quite frankly, the first seventy really sucked.

Creativity is a hard business and a very deliberate process, but it always begins on a foundation of honesty and the seven maxims presented in this chapter.

The Foundation of Creativity: Be Honest

Being a creative leader in the world of buzz requires you to be open and honest because buzz and word-of-mouth marketing only work when they are absolutely believable. If you're going to rename a town from Halfway to Half.com, be open and honest about your intentions. Say it straight. You're doing it to get attention. You're doing it to put the brand on the map. If people sense you're being misleading about your intentions or manipulative about how you treat them, they won't want to play ball with you.

Perhaps you've heard about actors hired to talk up the benefits of a certain brand at softball games or surreptitiously take some tourist photos with a latest model of a Brand X digital camera. Some call it undercover marketing. I'm all for being audacious and grabbing attention that will connect, in a positive way, to your brand. But I advise you never to be deceptive when it comes to buzz. Deceptiveness is a boomerang; if you're working to get buzz started, be honest from the get-go. (You'll read about the impact of negative buzz in chapter 15.)

The Seven Maxims for Discovering Buzz Creativity

There is, as I said, no easy answer to coming up with the perfect buzz solution for your situation. But there are some guidelines that will start you along the path to finding that solution. My Seven Maxims for Discovering Buzz Creativity are:

Maxim 1: Be Courageous—Demand Creativity of Yourself

Buzzmarketing is about causing a stir. The irony, however, was stated by John Philip Jones, who after twenty-five years with J. Walter Thompson said that "when an ad promises to cause a stir it will be rejected [by corporations]." Another way of saying what you've already read in these pages is that the traditionalists who run corporations are very uncomfortable with buzz ideas (until you've demonstrated a buzz solution that bowls them over).

It's important to understand clearly this basic fact: Seventy percent of your sales will come from 30 percent of your heavy user customers. If you're Dell Schanze, owner of Totally Awesome Computers, and you get lots of nasty letters from little old ladies for a radio commercial in which you talked about picking a booger out of your daughter's nose—you're not worried. Why? Because little old ladies aren't your heavy users. No problem with rubbing some people the wrong way; just make sure they're not your heavy users. The rest of 'em? Let 'em sizzle! Creating controversy stokes the fire and gets further word of mouth and news media coverage.

Bottom line: If you want great buzzmarketing, you've got to be courageous.

I confess that in my own careers I've often been courageous in demanding outrageous creativity . . . but on some occasions, I've been gun-shy.

Let's talk about gun-shy first and get it out of the way. If you're in an environment that doesn't take a lot of risks, you'll encounter a lot of see-mores. What's a see-more? Let me explain. You're trying to get consensus on a creative idea or execution—and nothing will move ahead because a few of the wimpy people will want to see more. As a result, you decrease emphasis on demanding the best possible creative work, and increase your emphasis on satisfying all the cooks in the kitchen. In that predicament, your marketing will be reduced to the lowest common vanilla denominator and you will stay invisible.

I've been there, and I've been caught without courage a few times in the past. How do you get around this dilemma? It's tough. Depending on your situation, you could go right to final execution (or near final execution). Produce the radio ad, create the final print ad, or whatever, because saying no to a finished product is harder than asking to see more. It's ready to go and no imagination is involved. Most of the time, it works.

Another way to combat the see-mores is to build consensus with all your cooks in the kitchen—but do it at the stage of defining the marketing problem. After you've built consensus on defining the marketing problem, narrow your list of cooks who you'll ask approval from on the final piece.

Now let's talk about being courageous in a culture where you have some greater latitude.

Rule number one is, if you want big ideas, be prepared to be uncomfortable. Big ideas will always make you uncomfortable in some respect. If you're comfortable, it's too vanilla. It's too invisible. You need to be a little uncomfortable.

But . . . it takes two to tango when demanding big, uncomfortable ideas.

You've got to be courageous enough to send the work back if

it's not the best—even if you're up against a deadline. It takes courage to risk deadlines. It takes courage to break through the clutter. It takes courage to be different. It takes courage to rub some people the wrong way. It takes courage to take the heat.

Just remember, if you're pleasing everybody, your advertising will look like everybody else's, and you'll be invisible.

If you're a buzzmarketer, you push buttons and start conversations. Some of those conversations may be negative (little old ladies and other non–heavy users). You've got to take the good with the bad because the impact of breaking through the clutter far outweighs following convention. Get heard or follow the herd.

Maxim 2: Define the Problem . . . Dump the Strategy

Dump strategy? That's pretty stupid, right? No way.

One of the reasons you want to dump the strategy is because of the word itself . . . *strategy*. The word *strategy* has been increasingly abused and overused since the 1980s. Even Mike Tyson knows: "It's great to have a strategy until you get hit in the head." When I worked at PepsiCo's Pizza Hut division, someone once said, "It's hard to be strategic when your ass is on fire!" The word itself has no real meaning now. It can be used as an adjective, an adverb, a verb, and a noun—and nowhere can it be used *in*correctly. When you use the word *strategic,* it sounds so impressive that it can't be used incorrectly. Any word loses meaning when it has neither correct nor incorrect application.

So dump the strategy!

The brilliant marketer Frank Delano put it best in his book *Brand Slam:*

Enough with strategies, strategies, and more strategies. Ball games are won when a player steps up to the plate and smacks one out of the ball park. There's no strategy for that . . .

So where do you start? By defining the problem.

What's the problem you want to solve? "Sell more cases," or "increase sales 15 percent"—no, no, no, that's a goal. The problem is usually much deeper. A problem is: eBay sells more computers online than anyone but nobody realizes it. That's a problem well defined.

Defining a problem accurately gives you direction.

A problem well defined is already half solved, because you discover direction.

Here's a literal example. If you're heading south, and discover you should be heading north, you waste a lot of effort and time getting back on course, because it's the opposite direction. But if you're heading north and discover you should be heading northeast, it's a lot easier to adjust—at least you were already moving in the right general direction.

The essence of creativity begins with understanding the marketing problem, defining the marketing problem, and heading in the right direction.

Maxim 3: Understand Your Consumers Firsthand

You can't be creative without knowing your consumer firsthand—meaning, in person, in real life. Secondary research is interesting, but it can be misleading. When Monica Lewinsky was in all the headlines, the American public told researchers they were sick of her and didn't want to hear any more about it. Yet 48 million tuned in to see her interviewed by Barbara Walters on *20/20,* setting a record.

What we say to researchers versus what we believe and do in real life can be extremely misleading. Roger Enrico said it pretty well: "You can't learn a damned thing if you spend all day in your own chair."

When I first assumed the marketing role at Pep Boys, my wife and I realized we'd need a third car for our live-in nanny. I looked at buying a used Toyota Camry or a big Oldsmobile Delta 88. I knew the Toyota would last, and be reliable. I knew the Olds would be fantastic on the highway but, with 118,000 miles on it, would break down more often. One of my goals, however, was to walk in the shoes of a Pep Boys consumer and experience what they experience. Pep Boys consumers owned older cars that broke down and needed repair. If I bought the Olds, I would be visiting Pep Boys a lot more than if I bought the Toyota. I bought the Olds.

I got what I asked for. A lot of stuff needed replacing on that car: timing chain, tie rods, tires, oxygen sensor, mass air-flow sensor, cam sensor, alternator, battery, heater core, hub bearing, and a lot more. A fair amount of mechanical issues, and lots of electrical issues. (Excuse me for interrupting the train of thought, but here's a word of advice about cars learned from hard experience: As soon as you start having electrical problems exceeding $400 in labor, things are only going to get worse—it's time to sell the junker.)

When advertising responsibilities were added to my marketing responsibilities at Pep Boys, one of the first things I did was bring the agency account team to Las Vegas . . . to work in the stores. We donned our uniforms, felt our customer's anxiety, solved our customer's problems, saw what they looked like, heard what they sounded like. We got under their hoods, and inside their heads.

Walk in the shoes of your customers, and you'll get invaluable sparks of creativity. You'll know your product better, you'll experience new emotions, and you'll find inspiration for new ideas. Walk in the shoes of the consumer, and you'll discover your own creative currency.

Maxim 4: Swing the Bat Often

To come up with big ideas, you've got to swing the bat often. The more you swing, the better your odds. Just don't settle—keep swinging.

When Henry Kissinger was secretary of state, he had to deliver a white paper on a particular foreign policy issue. Secretaries of state rarely write their own white papers . . . senior writers scribe the first versions. The senior writer for this topic did just that, and sent it to Kissinger for review. It came back with a note from Kissinger saying, "Not good enough." The writer hemmed and hawed in denial, but came to the realization that Kissinger was right. It was not his best work. The paper was rewritten and proudly resubmitted to Kissinger. It came back with another brief note from Kissinger saying, "Needs to be better." Again the writer sulked, but agreed it could be better. It was rewritten, resubmitted, and was summarily returned with yet another brief note of rejection. This back and forth took place five times.

On the sixth submission, Kissinger said, "Okay, now I'll read it." Then he read the white paper for the first time. With minor punctuation changes, it was completely acceptable.

To get the best work, Kissinger knew he had to swing the bat often. Talented, creative professionals produce excellent work and are not easily discouraged. But creativity that grabs you by the jock strap or bra strap is hard to produce. It may take all of those seventy tries to come up with the right idea, the right words, the right visual that grabs the consumer and won't let go. Creativity requires talent, but it also requires a lot of bat swings.

To get the best, you've got to be demanding. And that in itself takes courage.

Jimmy Johnson, former head coach of the Dallas Cowboys, demanded both discipline *and* creativity. He paid more attention to heart, soul, and emotion than to raw scores. Running forty yards in 4.2 seconds might have been impressive, but it didn't really matter to Jimmy Johnson. The most important thing he did to inspire his players was utter the words, "We need people to make big plays." He said it over and over and over.

Jimmy Johnson won two Super Bowls in five years. Of course he had talented players, but many a team fails even with great, very highly paid talent. Jimmy Johnson inspired his players, and pushed them to their creative limits. He was a leader—not just a coach.

In marketing, someone needs to take the Henry Kissinger and Jimmy Johnson roles. Indeed, marketing and advertising can be exciting and fun but creating word-of-mouth buzz, whether traditional or nontraditional, is draining, demanding, and frustrating. You pretty much know when you've nailed the Big Idea, but the hours and discipline involved in getting there can be excruciating.

Demand big ideas, demand big plays, and swing the bat often.

Maxim 5: Initiate Competition

Today, Budweiser is one of the most creative advertisers when it comes to creating word-of-mouth buzz through traditional media like TV. How do they do it? I think the answer lies in competition. Many years ago, Anheuser-Busch's Martin Weinberg calculated the probability of an ad agency coming up with a strong campaign: His estimate was one in twenty.

On top of that, he projected that the probability of Anheuser-Busch's management recognizing a strong campaign also averaged one in twenty (remember all those cooks in the kitchen!).

When you combine those two sets of probabilities, the odds of developing a campaign that could generate buzz average one in four hundred. At a rate of twenty commercials per year, it would take Anheuser-Busch decades to grab attention.

But they wanted to accelerate the odds of coming up with buzz-generating creativity. So what did they do?

They initiated competition. Unlike most advertising tradition, where one agency handles all the creative work, Anheuser-Busch assigned its creative work to two agencies, Goodby Silverstein and DDB (both owned by the same parent company, Omnicom).

Without a doubt, one of the key reasons that Budweiser is now producing buzz-generating creativity is because of the rivalry between two strong agencies. As an Anheuser-Busch marketing executive explained, "The one-upmanship factor produces much better creative . . . a little competition is healthy and encourages the cream to [rise to] the top."

My prediction is that we'll see more and more of these competitive arrangements for marketers wanting to get optimum return for their ad dollars. Sure, that competition can make a deep dent in your ad budget—you pay twice for the same job. But the risk of being invisible may cost you even more.

Another Perspective on Demanding Creativity

I asked two advertising agencies to provide their perspectives on creativity. Both agencies are, in my opinion, among the boldest in the industry. They create work that breaks loose from the rest of the pack.

Here are a few of their thoughts on creativity.

CRISPIN PORTER + BOGUSKY

When Crispin Porter + Bogusky go to work for a brand, they begin with one overarching mission: "How are we going to make this brand famous?"

Notice that they don't begin with something like, "What's the media plan?" They want to make brands famous. Because it's well-recognized brands that people talk about. Famous brands automatically get more media attention. Famous brands get ten news impressions for every one advertising impression.

Let me say it again: Famous brands get ten news impressions for every one advertising impression.

Jeff Hicks, president of the ad agency Crispin Porter + Bogusky (CP+B), told us they demand advertising that creates buzz. But not just for the sake of creating interest. According to CP+B, the advertising must establish buzz in a way that logically connects with the brand—by connecting with what the brand stands for. (Remember my warning against being outrageous for the sake of pure outrageousness!)

When CP+B put And1 (a popular basketball shoe brand) on the map, they blazed an entirely new trail for the line. They avoided the pitfall of trying to make a brand famous by following the path the giant shoe companies were taking.

At the time, giants like Nike and Adidas were all about big business athletics. Although CP+B takes research seriously, with a Ph.D. on staff, most of their research efforts center around in-person anthropology. For And1, they performed dozens of in-depth, one-on-one consumer interviews; focus groups are a no-no. CP+B prefers to operate in one-on-one settings, and those settings aren't always in a conference room. Their people went to consumers' homes and went into their bedrooms, looking for what pictures were on their walls, and what particular pages had been torn out of magazines and pinned above their beds. The agency wanted to see how the basketball-shoe consumer lived, breathed, ate, and slept.

What CP+B discovered was that they'd be wise not to follow the NBA path. They found consumers jaded by NBA salaries, jaded by NBA success, and jaded by NBA endorsements. Their target buyers identified more with "street ball" basketball than with NBA basketball. And Nike owned the NBA angle, anyway. So And1 set out to discover brand roots it could own and grow with.

They found those roots in street ball, and CP+B chose to blaze a new trail rooted in that aspect of the sport. Pursuing that direction put And1 on the map. Sales more than tripled, exceeding $200 million per year, and the brand went from the number-five-selling basketball sneaker to the number-two-selling basketball sneaker—second only to Nike.

Another creative philosophy that makes CP+B unique is their approach to media. The company begins with the premise that everything is media. Everything. Most important, the ideas come first and the channels for media come only after the ideas are set.

Why limit yourself to a particular canvas of thirty-second TV spots?

You may have seen some of this agency's work when BMW launched the Mini Cooper. CP+B created buzz because of some entirely new visuals, mentioned later (chapter 15), such as the huge SUV with a Mini strapped on the top. Or the *Playboy* centerfold featuring a Mini. Significantly, the Mini was launched with one-fifth the budget of the VW Beetle. On a smaller budget, CP+B used big buzz, not big budget, to realize a lot more bang for the buck.

Of course, their client list is growing rapidly and now includes recognized brands like Burger King (campaigns creating buzz such as SubservientChicken.com). But this agency intends to continue thinking like innovators—dedicated to making brands famous for a fraction of the cost.

Deutsch

Not many agencies are as bold as Deutsch, an agency that consistently produces some of the nation's most talked about creative work for clients like Mitsubishi, DirecTV, Snapple, and California Cheese. It's lauded as one of the most creative agencies in the country and has been named Agency of the Year for five years' running by *Adweek* magazine.

And during an economic period when most ad agencies have been shrinking along with the economy, Deutsch has been rewarded with explosive growth—because this agency has been embracing the elephant in the room that 90 percent of all agencies don't want to talk about. What's the elephant in the room?

Sales results.

Deutsch understands that the ultimate goal of advertising is to move the sales needle into positive territory. Advertising is not about winning awards for beauty and cleverness, nor is about pumping egos. Its measurement of success is sales.

Of course, some agencies you talk to will eventually get around to mentioning sales, but in my experience, it's not a topic they want to talk about too soon. Most don't even bring it up. But Deutsch has been embracing it and professing it from the tallest mountains. As Deutsch managing director Eric Hirshberg put it:

> *We pray equally to both gods. The god of artistic excellence and the god of results. We're intensely focused on great creative by making human connections with people.*
>
> *But that must be coupled with the force of selling product. Advertising that wins awards but doesn't sell product provokes a clash of values between clients and ad agencies that is impossible to bridge.*
>
> *To be great **commercial** art, it has to be both: commercial, **and** art. If it doesn't get results, it wasn't great advertising. Period. It might have been great something else, comedy, entertainment, etc. But great advertising has to make shit happen.*

Deutsch makes the distinction between art and commercial art. Art can make you feel good. Art in advertising can win you compliments at Christmas parties. But advertising is a form of commercial art—and commercial art has a clear purpose. If commercial art doesn't make the cash register ring, Deutsch believes it's not great advertising.

Making human connections through creative excellence coupled with making sales grow is a difficult balance. Mitsubishi wanted that particular balance when Deutsch was given the task of resurrecting the Mitsubishi brand. At the time Mitsubishi approached Deutsch, sales were in serious decline. Mitsubishi was doing so poorly that analysts began to speculate that the company would pack up and exit the country.

Deutsch began its approach by discovering the true soul of the Mitsubishi product line and by discovering how cars make people feel. The Mitsubishi product was wrapped in flashy curves and aggressive styling. It was somewhat adolescent, with a hint of Hot Wheels.

But the Mitsubishi product didn't make people feel anything one way or another. Certain car brands are able to elicit a specific response from many people. For example, buying a Toyota might make a person feel smart yet not ostentatious. A Honda might appeal to people who like to experience simple solutions.

Deutsch knew that Mitsubishi couldn't out-Toyota Toyota or out-Honda Honda. Instead, it focused on consumers likely to consider brands other than Toyota or Honda. The agency searched until it found a consumer segment likely to switch to Mitsubishi—people desiring fashion with an edge of vanity.

So fashion-with-an-edge-of-vanity became the common ground and the soul of the Mitsubishi ads. These very human feelings appealed to this very likely target audience. While Toyota and Honda made cars and advertising that talked to people's intelligence, the new campaign created for Mitsubishi talked to consumers' emotions.

As Deutsch's advertising reached into the heart of the matter, things began moving. At this writing, Mitsubishi sales are up 89 percent, dealer profits are up a whopping 300 percent, and all is looking up.

The interesting part about the Mitsubishi advertising is its buzz phenomenon. The car is in many ways marketed like a fashion product. And by setting trends, the ads, as well as the products, have become buzz.

Most products borrow from buzz and weave it into their marketing. For example, the Windows 95 launch from Microsoft borrowed the Rolling Stones' "Start Me Up" and proceeded to squash IBM's OS/2 from the market. Marlboro's famous Marlboro Country campaign borrowed music from the popular movie *The Magnificent Seven*. Even Apple's 1984 commercial borrowed buzz (from George Orwell's Big Brother phenomenon). Not that there's anything wrong with that—we've been talking about it in our previous four secrets!

But what Deutsch is doing with its fashion-like marketing of Mitsubishi proves to be a groundbreaking form of buzz. A big component of the campaign revolves around music—which makes the human connection with the target. Deutsch, though, is introducing hip, undiscovered music, an idiom very appealing to both the boomers and the Gen Xers.

In a typical buzz model, people are the introducers of buzz. Deutsch's campaign, in contrast, is making the Mitsubishi brand the good guys—as introducers of new music groups. Just as Halston was looking for the next undiscovered thing that would generate buzz, Deutsch is looking for the next undiscovered band that will create buzz for Mitsubishi.

Ask radio disc jockeys how the song, "Start the Commotion" became the center of interest; they all know that it got started in "those great Mitsubishi ads." Ask DJs how bands like Dirty Vegas got buzz and they all know. Although musicians once were leery about licensing their music to advertising, Deutsch and its Mitsubishi ads have become recognized as the introducers of buzz. Undiscovered bands profit from it, but Mitsubishi holds the currency. Bands now inundate Deutsch with demo tapes, hoping to be featured in the next release of Mitsubishi currency.

Consequently, the Mitsubishi brand becomes even more interesting. And the Mitsubishi brand by way of its music buzz becomes the center of interest in our music-oriented culture.

In the halls of Deutsch, not only will you hear the next new, undiscovered music of pop culture, you'll hear a lot of discussion about religion, commitment, and value systems. A commitment to selling product, and a commitment to commercial art. A value system that distinguishes between art, which is without boundaries, and commercial art, which has boundaries and is problem-solving by nature.

This is where Deutsch breaks away from the pack in many respects. I've encountered a substantial number of agencies rooted in art, energized by being able to create without boundaries. But when you have no boundaries, it's hard to focus on sales and commercial purpose. Commercial art, though, has boundaries and purpose. Deutsch not only understands that there will be boundaries but embraces the boundaries as part of its value system.

When client and agency have the same value system and commitment, they find themselves sitting on the same side of the table. And when client and advertiser sit on the same side of the table, they are far more likely to produce breakaway advertising.

For Deutsch, the commitment, the religion, and the value system are much more important than industry awards. For them, it's not about the *a*wards, it's about the *re*wards.

Maxim 6: Pay Attention to Names and Words

This may sound obvious, but sometimes what's obvious gets overlooked anyway.

Pay attention to names and words. Phonetics, rhyme, meter, and alliteration are amazingly important.

Which sounds like more fun to you: Ultimate TV or TiVo? AltaVista or Google? Billpoint or PayPal? Lycos or Yahoo? Gooseberry or Kiwi? March playoffs or March Madness?

There are certain words that are just fun to say: "Banana" is a fun word. "Kiwi" is a fun word. "Google" is a fun word. "Yahoo" is a fun word.

So what's the point?

When it comes to buzzmarketing—getting people to talk about your brand—people are far more likely to talk about your brand if the name is fun to say.

Where is Ultimate TV? Although it was backed by Microsoft's huge marketing dollars, it did not get buzz. TiVo, on the other hand, did get buzz. No big marketing budget whatsoever, but it had a name that was fun to say. It got people talking; it got buzz.

When OverweightDate.com started, the name was different. As soon as it switched to OverweightDate, people started talking about it because it was fun to say, because it rhymes.

When the gooseberry first came to America . . . oops, what's a gooseberry? In New Zealand, what we call kiwifruit was until 1959 called the Chinese gooseberry. To importers, the name "gooseberry" had other connotations: Was it an egg laid by a goose? Was it some strange New Zealand virus? The name was changed to kiwi, and it found a place in the American market. More fun to say, more fun to eat.

Phonetics matters a lot. Welsh poet Dylan Thomas is probably most famous for the poem "Do Not Go Gentle Into That Good Night." One of the observed subtexts that makes this poem so effective is that the phonetics actually slows you down. Phonetically it is very hard to have *N*'s and *T*'s together, or *D*'s and *N*'s together. The phonetics achieves what the poem calls for; it slows you down by making the words difficult to pronounce.

When you're creating marketing, do the exact opposite: Make it easy to say; let it roll off their tongues.

Maxim 7: Create Content, Not Ads

When people mention the word *advertising* to Kerri Martin, the head of marketing for the Mini, she promptly corrects them. "Not advertising," she says. "Creative content." Mini and its agency CP+B don't produce ads, they produce creative content. It may end up in a particular format commonly known as an ad, but in an over-saturated advertising world where the majority of people don't pay attention to ads . . . what people do pay attention to is content.

In common with *American Idol,* the *Crossroads* movie, wacky people dressed up in homemade French's Potato Sticks costumes, and Dell Schanze of Totally Awesome Computers, Kerri Martin and her marketers create content, not ad copy.

We want to be entertained and engaged—not sold to. Right now, more and more companies are buying two-minute (and longer) time slots on TV, showing short films with their products woven into them. Why? People pay attention to content, not ads—and smart brands are recognizing this and weaving their brand into content instead of creating ads.

Companies are moving away from strict radio ads, and teaming up with companies like MatrixMediaInc. and UBC Radio Network to produce entire radio and TV shows where the advertiser pays for the show and for its distribution. Cooking shows, automotive shows, health and fitness shows, any show imaginable. *TV Guide* works with them to produce a ninety-second rundown of what's on TV tonight—with a sponsored marketing message embedded. Craig Ferguson's highlights from the previous night are brought to you in a sixty-second piece of content—with a sponsored marketing message embedded. Radio ads are going out of favor, because people will push their preset button or make a cell phone call as soon as they know a block of ads are coming, but they won't do that with content. As long as it entertains and engages, people will pay attention to content.

Ads get impressions, but content makes connections.

Recap

The first four secrets of buzzmarketing are focused on understanding what can generate buzz and how that happens. This fifth secret, discovering the best possible creativity, deals with finding the ideas that will generate buzz.

Discovering creativity is hard. It's a draining, deliberate process that requires pouring your soul into the search for ideas that can result in breakaway growth. Courage is required every step of the way.

But whether you're a big brand or a small start-up, you're all equal when it comes to creativity. Nobody has a monopoly on talent and nobody holds a monopoly on creativity.

If you demand big ideas, you'll get big ideas.

If you want great ideas and can feel it in your soul; if you have the courage to take risks; and if you've developed the needed persistence to swing the bat often, you will hit the buzz ball out of the stadium.

You can do it!

CHAPTER FIFTEEN

Mustang Bang

Isn't discovering creativity easier for small start-ups than for big brands? After all, a start-up has less to lose, right?

Think again. Whether big or small, competitors are out there aiming to eat your lunch every single day. There's no monopoly on discovering creativity. Here's how Mustang discovered it.

Between 1961 and 1964, two out of three Americans looking for a new car didn't even consider a Ford. The company had lost several points of market share and, although it had some bright spots, it was using its automotive powers in all the wrong ways—essentially driving itself right off a cliff.

The brand had such low equity that Lee Iacocca, then the company's general manager, was even making the case for removing the Ford blue oval from its Galaxie model. (This, needless to say, didn't go over well with Henry Ford II, who responded, "Do you know whose name is on the God-damned building!") To consumers, Ford was tired and dull.

The launch of the Mustang on April 17, 1964, would change that perception forever, and ignite one of the most amazing business turnarounds in history. Even the market leader, GM, couldn't touch the Mustang's success; many said its competing vehicle, the

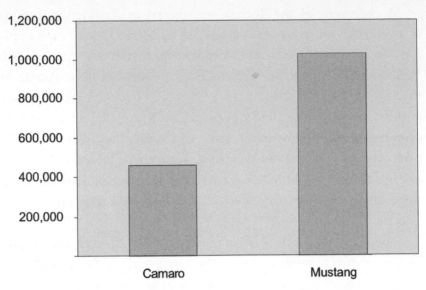

Mustangs and Camaros Sold in First Two Years After Mustang Introduction

Chevrolet Camaro, was a better car. But Mustang prevailed—outselling Camaro by a two to one margin.

What's in a Name?

It began life as the T-5 project, and was launched in 1961 in a locked, austere conference room of Ford's Buhl Building called The Tomb. Fewer than ten executives from Ford and three from its ad agency, J. Walter Thompson, had keys to get in. All waste paper was burned, taking no chance of a leak. Not even cleaning people had access to The Tomb.

The project was Lee Iacocca's baby, and he was demanding nothing less than a youthful sports car that looked like no other. The result, in June 1963, was an Italian-looking sports car, curiously named after a town in Italy.

A prototype of the Torino was shown in confidence to consumers. Fifty-two couples were invited to Detroit to give their opinions on the new prototype. Despite excited anticipation from the Torino team, the reaction wasn't exactly overwhelming. People in the test group liked the car for what it was but thought it was, of all things, "too fancy." They guessed the price to be 35 to 40 percent higher than it actually was. And when they were told the price, they simply did not believe it. Were they pleased to hear the car would cost so little? No way; they were suspicious, figuring something must be wrong with a car that seemed so good but cost so little.

The good news was that the design itself had broad appeal. The bad news was that something still didn't add up for consumers. And that's a serious flaw: Never puzzle your consumer.

To address the issue of consumer confusion, the J. Walter Thompson team pleaded to change the vehicle's name. Earlier, they had come up with the name Mustang; when the Ford execs had dismissed the idea, it created some dissent. Now the question of the car's name resurfaced. At the eleventh hour, the brand name was changed. The car would be called Mustang.

And none too soon. At this point, the TV commercials and print ads had been shot with the car badged as the Torino. Everything would have to be redone with the now-famous Mustang emblem—reshooting all the commercials at considerable expense, and with little time left.

The Seed of Buzz

Seven months earlier, when the task of marketing the new car was handed to the J. Walter Thompson advertising team, Iacocca had taken the unusual step of giving the ad agency full license. Their only direction was: Be creative. Be different. Be spectacular. Be thorough.

Walter Mead, chief creative director of J. Walter Thompson, re-called much later how rare it was, over the course of an entire ad-vertising career, to be allowed to "go for broke" as they were on the Mustang launch. This level of creative freedom led Norman Strouse, then president of the agency, in a new direction, one that advocated a "far closer liaison between promotion, publicity, and advertis-ing." The philosophy would influence the way Ford would go to market with the Mustang and would shape how the Mustang's ap-peal would be built—on buzz.

After much research and taking full advantage of the license to go for broke, Mead presented the creative cornerstone of Mus-tang's marketing. It was titled "Everyone Wants to Be Someone of Consequence." It outlined what was later referred to as the "Walter Mitty campaign."

One print ad showed the Mustang, a dowdy-looking man, and a pretty girl. Beneath this picture, the copy read:

> *Two weeks ago this man was a bashful schoolteacher in a small midwestern city. Add Mustang. Now he has three steady girls, is on first name terms with the best headwaiter in town, and is society's darling. All the above came with his Mustang . . .*

Similar types of tongue-in-cheek ads were used with the librar-ian, Penelope Sweezy, who turned into a voluptuous attention-getter . . . once she got her Mustang.

The Walter Mitty–themed advertising ran in print, and on TV. Americans knew it was tongue-in-cheek and chuckled along. The people at Ford and the agency were surprised at the letters that started pouring in from men and women across America describing their own attention-getting transformation once behind the wheel of their Mustang. Even eighty-year-old women wrote Ford describ-ing how they were now getting more looks from the boys. The brand was positioned as "class for the mass"—very similar to today's Target stores, with their "good fashion for the masses" approach.

Mustang was marketing itself as more than a new automobile. It was a new way of life.

Buzz

The seeds of buzz were sewn with the Walter Mitty ads, and the marketing campaign that launched the Mustang created national hysteria. *Newsweek* reported in April 1964 that "Americans would have to be deaf, dumb, and blind to avoid the name."

The advertising of the new Mustang was an event in itself. Rather than simply launch the Mustang campaign, Ford teased the debut. It used newspaper ads in America's top sixty markets to advertise upcoming TV commercials. The ads boldly read, "The most exciting thing on TV tonight will be a commercial . . . get your first look at the year's most exciting new car . . . the new Ford Mustang. Tonight, 9:30." It was, in effect, advertising its advertising—even before the product had hit the market.

For the first time ever, Ford bought all the TV advertising time between 9:30 and 10:00 P.M. on a Thursday night to saturate America with the first announcement of the new car. *All* of the advertising time. Whatever channel you were watching, the advertising you saw was Mustang's. Today, there's a term for it; Ford and the agency had invented what's now called the "roadblock."

The advance advertising building up to that night teased the nation with news of the "secret" that was about to be unveiled. If you tuned in at 9:30 P.M. on Thursday, you'd be one of the first to discover it. This approach spurred nationwide curiosity and tremendous anticipation. Seventy-five percent of America tuned in that night.

The tactic of creating a nationwide roadblock was a first ever— which itself became news. Soon after the first TV announcements, the country was blanketed with 15,500 billboards announcing that the secret was out.

The company also unleashed the most innovative radio advertising campaign of its kind. Ford bought substantial advertising time from radio stations employing the top two hundred DJs in America—on one condition. The DJs must come to Detroit, test drive the car on Ford's proving grounds before the launch, and write their own copy for the sixty-second ad, talking about their Mustang test drive.

The DJs were also given a Mustang for a week in their home market through local dealers. One DJ was so insulted that he *wasn't* invited to participate as one of the top two hundred DJs in the country that he created his own voluntary campaign to get back at Ford. His negative radio commercial was titled, "How I brought Ford Motor Company to its knees." The story of the jealous DJ made national headlines. He was eventually invited to participate as DJ number 201, and was given his Mustang for a week. Inevitably, the Mustang got far more play than the radio time purchased. Through its innovative and bold marketing campaign, Mustang literally became the talk of the town.

Stampede

The day after the launch, a Chicago dealership had to lock its doors because too many people were crowding into the dealership. In Huntsville, Alabama, nine thousand people at a stock car race jumped a retaining wall to see the new Mustang being prepared as the pace car. Within days of the launch, Ford dealers wrote up sales for twenty-two thousand Mustangs, and the Mustang plants developed a three-month backlog.

In the first several months, four million people swarmed into Ford dealerships. Four *million*.

Both *Time* and *Newsweek* featured Ford and Iacocca on their covers during the week of launch. The Mustang hysteria that swept the nation, and the backlog of orders, became news itself. Even editorial writers jumped into the frenzy, churning out features on the Mustang that appeared in twenty-one of the major market newspapers. The publicity value was pegged at $10 million, in 1964 dollars (approximately $100 million in today's dollars).

Print ads for the Mustang scored an almost unheard of 95 percent readership. Why? Because people were actually reading the advertising. They wanted to know what all the buzz was about. When buzz and advertising coincide, the impact of advertising is six to ten times more effective.

And Ford knew how to build on buzz. In fact, it began making ads about it. One ad highlighted the company's network of seven thousand dealerships. Its headline read, "How to Make 7,000 Grown Men Cry," and depicted the Mustang launch overwhelming dealers with orders they couldn't fill. Another ad featured a crowd of people surrounding the Mustang all talking about the car:

One person is saying, "I gotta have it, I gotta have it!" A woman indicating the Mustang owner says, "Who does *he* work for?"

A man says, "Under $2,500?"

Another man exalts, "Yeah!"

A woman walking by says, "Imagine! Grown men acting like schoolboys over a *car!*"

Ads like this showed a keen understanding of its market, and showed the willingness of the Ford people to laugh at themselves a little.

The Mustang proved to be a conversation starter, and Ford created even more buzz with ads that were about the very buzz Mustang created—adding fuel to the fire. In less than 150 days, Mustang sold 100,000 cars. In its first year, Mustang sold more than 418,000 cars and could have sold more if capacity allowed. Before its second anniversary, Mustang sold more than one million cars, capturing 5 percent of the entire car market with just one model.

The Emperor Has No Clothes

Although Mustang had a handsome exterior, the car itself really wasn't all that special. One writer from the *New York Journal-American* wrote, "When I drove a Mustang for the first time . . . I said to my Ford friends, that I honestly wasn't very impressed with its performance."

Not as many writers would be so candid. After all, what newspaper would want to slow the stampede of Mustang buzz? What writer would want to cast aspersions on American innovation? Who would want to bring down the transformation of Penelope Sweezy, the dowdy librarian who was now "someone of consequence"? It all cut too close to criticizing the American dream.

But perhaps it wouldn't have mattered even if more reporters and car critics had spoken out. Two years after the Mustang launch, GM introduced its competitive car, the Camaro. By most accounts, Camaro was equal to Mustang in design, form, and function. In fact, by many accounts it was a far superior car to Mustang.

Camaro couldn't touch Mustang. But GM sure tried.

GM offered consumers a great product and spent almost double the advertising dollars of Mustang, but the public didn't bite. Camaro was positioned more as a muscle car, and its marketing was vanilla. And vanilla captures no buzz.

Mustang, however, continued to charge along quite nicely, even making its way into pop culture. In 1966, Wilson Pickett topped the music charts with his song "Mustang Sally." In 1968, a Steve McQueen movie, *Bullitt,* featured a Mustang car chase lasting eight minutes—still heralded as one of the most famous car chases in American movie history. Lee Iacocca even walked by a bakery one day and read a sign promoting hot cakes that claimed, "They're selling like Mustangs."

By all rational accounts, Camaro sales should have at least equaled Mustang's. Camaro was a faster car and considered in many ways better. The Mustang success surpassed all rational explanation. It was built on buzz, not on a chassis. From the very beginning, and throughout a three-decade journey, it would outsell Camaro by a very wide margin.

A Mini Revolution

Looking at modern-day automobiles, few have created Mustang-style buzz. Saturn has come close, with its industry-breaking "no haggle" buying experience. The Volkswagen Beetle captured attention with its cute design, but sales have slumped from 81,000 units a year to the 50,000 range (now boosted by its convertible model).

But in terms of pure personality, keeping manufacturing capacity at 100 percent, and overall buzz, look no farther than Mini.

What is it about the Mini that's different from the Beetle or the Saturn? A lot. But when you boil it down, the success behind the Mini can be attributed to one thing: tons of personality.

More Than Clever Ads

The challenge to introduce Mini to the American market was a big one. Not only did it have to launch a car model, it had to launch an entire brand. No dealerships existed in the United States, and awareness ranked at 10 percent (versus 90 percent awareness in the UK). Another part of the problem was that Mini's name hinted at its marketing budget—tiny, by automotive standards. Mini's first-year budget was a paltry one-fifth of the Beetle's launch. That meant no big TV campaign—in fact, no TV at all.

What Mini did do with their small-budget campaign, though, was similar to Mustang. Like Mustang, Mini was selling more than just a car. The Mustang ad about the schoolteacher had said it all: Tongue in cheek. No hard sell. Gobs of personality.

Mini went the same route with its clever advertising. The collector's edition of *The New Yorker* with the series of Mini cartoons. The centerfold of the Mini in *Playboy* magazine. Mini in the seats of four football stadiums. The humongous SUV with a Mini strapped to its roof driving around twenty-two cities for seven weeks. The test drive on the *Today* show, where Al Roker and the Naked Cowboy tooled around Manhattan. While the campaign was brilliant, the Mini is "a lot more than clever advertising," says the marketing honchette behind it all, Kerri Martin.

Personality

I hope you'll take many ideas and concepts away from this book, but if you remember one word and one word only, remember *personality*. Mini exemplifies it.

What's so special about personality? Without it, products can certainly still succeed, but they lack consumer passion—a driving goal in creating buzz, marketing, branding, and buying. But meditate for a while on the brands that people passionately talk about, and you'll discover that almost all of them possess personality—a human quality. They resemble a corporation far less than they do a person. A person you would enjoy spending time with.

Contrast these brands:

Corporate Brands	Personality Brands
HP	Apple Computer
Microsoft	Google
Breyers	Ben & Jerry's
Pontiac	VW Beetle
uBid	eBay

Certainly HP, Microsoft, and the others are successful companies, if you define success by distribution, competitive advantage, product quality, innovation, design, and employees. But expand that definition a bit to include brand loyalty, likeability, and personality, and they come up lacking.

In addition to buzz, Mustang, too, had personality—a lot of which was created simply through advertising. Whimsical, self-deprecating, and approachable. More like a person, less like a corporation. And Mini follows suit.

Mini exudes personality. Yes, the Beetle exuded personality, too, but it didn't quite carry over to the dealership and every single experience and touch point (point of contact). Read the bible of the Mini (the Manual of Motoring) and you'll discover that Mini's personality extends far beyond the sheet metal into every possible area. It's a brand that's clever, not afraid to joke, not afraid to laugh at itself; and again, far more like a person than a corporation. In this quirky bible of motoring, Mini says, "It is your duty to give your Mini a name befitting its unique personality."

And according to motoring advisor Julie Hoffman, 75 percent of all Mini owners actually do name their car, while 60 percent customize their car, too, with the more than two hundred different options available. In fact, people are individualizing their Minis to the point that it would be rare to find two Minis exactly the same.

Anthropomorphize. You'll hear this word (yes, it's a mouthful) used by many at Mini dealerships and headquarters. The definition: to give human qualities to. When it comes to the vehicle itself, Mini wants to transform a slab of metal into a member of your family—one with personality. You may not always talk about your car, but you're likely to talk about a car you've customized, that you've named and, perhaps, that you even talk to. Like Harley owners, they're a little fanatical.

But Mini's personality doesn't end with the car. It continues with the salespeople, or "motoring advisors," right from the moment they go in for training. First of all, they stay at a W—a fun and hip hotel chain that makes the Marriott look like grandma's house. Then their training is presented as a series of games—"edutainment instead of traditional lecturing and sleep-inducing slide presentations. The company carries its message through from beginning to end. And that message? Mini's got so much personality, it's coming out of its exhaust pipes.

Recap

When the first Minis rolled off the production line, there was something wrong. By American standards, the cup holder was way too small. But instead of letting it slide—after all, just because people couldn't fit their vente lattes in the holder didn't mean they weren't buying the car—Mini sent every owner a stainless steel cup holder with an apology note stating they understood that the cup holder wasn't sufficient, and please accept this as acknowledgment of that oversight in the first models. From a cost standpoint, no marketer would ever do this—far too expensive by most marketing standards. It was a way to capitalize on a sticky situation . . . and personalize it, too.

But that's how Mini performs on every level. Its branding isn't the logo or the ads alone. Mini understands that the sum of all experiences and touch points for customers is what matters. When it comes to marketing and branding, it's not the number of impressions that counts—it's the number of connections. Advertising, in its conventional sense, usually doesn't connect. When you connect with a human being, that's far more valuable than tallying up thousands of advertising impressions that go unnoticed.

The Mustang also succeeded with only half the budget put behind GM's Camaro, because it connected with people. Mustang connected personally with 201 radio DJs like no other advertiser ever did, giving them the buzz currency to become connected to the brand. The media became connected to it and fell in love with the Mustang. When it comes right down to it, advertising impressions don't count. Connections count.

Brands like Mini and Mustang succeed mostly because everything about their brands relates to people, not corporations. And we connect with people, not corporations.

Branding in the corporate style will be a thing of the past. Branding in the human style will be a thing of the future.

But branding alone isn't enough. There is one other essential element. Turn the page for the sixth and most important secret of all.

CHAPTER SIXTEEN

The Sixth Secret— Police Your Product

Policing your product is essential to buzz. It's the lifeblood of buzz. You need to deliver a product or service that wows people and continues to wow them, that works the way people expect it to work, that's backed up by an appropriate level of support. You need a product people will go out of their way to talk about. Without all that, you have no buzz.

All fifteen chapters you've read so far mean absolutely *nothing* if you don't eat, live, and breathe policing your product.

Victor Kiam—many people will remember the name. He was, before his death, the chairman of the board for Remington Products, and you might remember seeing him on television, selling his company's Remington shavers. Kiam used to say that the first rule of marketing is to have a great product. The second rule of marketing, he said, was: "Don't ever forget the first rule."

Anyone can get attention for a product. You can create a ready-made story for consumers and the media, and maybe you can even start conversations. Those are the very basics to take off with buzz.

A Recent Ride Down Product Quality Lane

Look at the VW Beetle and you'll discover lots of buzz, but a short ride. Two reasons why its journey stopped short: lack of exclusivity, and poor product quality.

The quality problems that plagued both the Beetle and VW in general ended its buzz, and sales plummeted. With any new and unusual product, you start with the advantage of novelty, but ultimately the proof of staying power is in the product's utility and quality. VW's quality failed miserably, and sales have sunk more than 35 percent since its buzz peak in 2000.

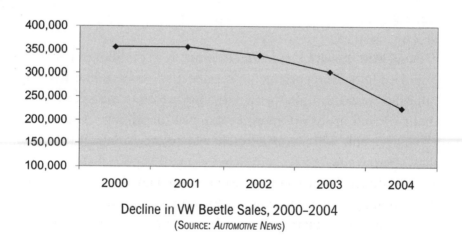

Decline in VW Beetle Sales, 2000–2004
(SOURCE: AUTOMOTIVE NEWS)

VW: Learn from Them, Don't Follow Them

In 2000, VW was riding on top of the world. The Beetle had propelled VW back into the spotlight with nostalgia, innovation, and clever advertising. The company racked up a sales record of 355,000 vehicles in one year.

Now turn to the quality issue. Fast-forward to the 2004 J. D.

Power Initial Quality Survey. Among all car brands, VW was placed second to last for initial quality in the entire auto industry!

Consumer Reports magazine removed the VW Jetta, Golf, and Beetle from its recommended list, and VW had to offer $3,000 incentives to sell vehicles—six times higher than previous incentive amounts.

While stopped at a traffic light, I spotted a VW with 8½-by-11-inch signs taped to the inside of its windows reading, "Don't EVER buy a VW, they are lemons," and "VW dealers stink—can't fix a car and treat you like dirt." In the driver's seat I saw a mild-mannered suburban housewife with graying hair, calmly waiting for the light to turn green. Those two hand-lettered signs, which cost her less than ten cents to make, probably did more damage to VW than they realized—offsetting the sales power of millions of dollars in advertising in slick magazines.

Recently, though, Len Hunt from the Audi division (11th of 37 in three-year quality) has taken over at VW. Believe me, Len has painfully learned a thing or two about the impact of bad product quality and the power of negative word of mouth.

When Audi's S4 turned up with a valve-spring problem in 2003, Hunt barked at executives in Germany to fix it fast. The German execs wanted to know, What's the big deal? It's "only a handful of cases." Hunt responded that it was all over the Internet, and 100,000 people were chatting about it.

What Len Hunt saw firsthand at Audi was the importance of a quality product and the devastation of bad buzz in today's world of rapid communications on the Web, WiFi, WiMax, and wireless.

The Statistics on Bad Buzz

Negative word of mouth—bad buzz—
spreads much faster than positive buzz.

Consider these statistics on the velocity of bad buzz:

⋮   23 complaints = 10,000 enemies   ⋮

For every twenty-three unhappy customers who take the time to complain to you, your company will have ten thousand enemies who didn't bother to write or call. Chances are you'll never hear a word of complaint from those additional ten thousand people. But they vote with their wallets.

According to an extensive research study conducted by Technical Research Programs in Washington, D.C., for every single complaint you get, there are twenty-six more unhappy customers who never bother to complain. On average, those twenty-six you never heard from will tell sixteen other people about your awful product.

> The impact of 23 complaining customers:
> For every one complaining customer,
> 26 customers who don't bother to
> complain = 27 unhappy customers.
> 27 unhappy customers x 16 people they
> will tell = 432 enemies (for every one complainer).
> 23 complaints x 432 enemies = 9,936 enemies
> (for every 23 complaints).

But these are the old stats from the days prior to the birth of the Web, WiFi, WiMax, and wireless. Today, those technologies have probably tripled the velocity of bad buzz.

Bad Buzz and Movie Statistics

How many times has this happened to you?

You're watching TV and see a new film advertised. The trailer causes you to salivate—you can't wait to see this one. On opening day you're lined up with a slew of others.

Two hours later you walk out unsatisfied. You estimate you got two bucks worth of entertainment from your $10 movie ticket. Where do you go for a refund? Who do you complain to?

You can't get a refund. But you can complain to all your friends—in fact, they see you as a hero for saving them $10. Today, thanks to electronic technology, bad buzz accelerates faster than an F-16 with afterburners ignited.

Five years ago, the average audience drop-off between a summer movie's opening weekend and its second weekend was 40 percent. Today, the average audience drop-off for a movie's second weekend sinks 18 percent lower than that.

Rick Sands, COO of Miramax Films, thinks that having a quality product is essential in every business. In the old days, he said, "there used to be a term, 'buying your gross.' You could buy your gross for the weekend and then overcome bad word of mouth because it took time for the news to spread out into the general audience."

With the rise of technology, it takes virtually no time for bad word of mouth to reach the general audience. Forget about second weekend drop-off, after the first Friday night of a movie's release, wireless phones start ringing immediately after the movie—especially since most wireless minutes are free after 9:00 P.M. and on weekends.

Hollywood marketers make amazing trailers—in some cases with more pizzazz than the movie itself. But they can no longer buy their gross revenues with marketing. Just like with VW, the days of trying to cover up a bad product with clever marketing are gone. Now more than ever, people put more faith in word of mouth and less faith in polished marketing.

Want more data on the importance of policing your product to ensure quality?

Doubletree Hotels—More Than Double Trouble

One fall evening, two weary businessmen from the information consulting firm Zaaz were traveling from Seattle to Houston for a meeting. They knew they would arrive late at night so they reserved their rooms with credit cards for guaranteed late arrival. After many typical travel delays, they arrived tired and cranky at their Doubletree Hotel; it was 2:00 in the morning and they had to be ready for an 8:00 A.M. meeting.

Much to their astonishment, the night clerk didn't seem to understand the true meaning of *guaranteed late arrival.* He had sold their rooms out from under them three hours earlier. When the businessmen asked why he had done such a thing, the response they got was shocking. "I have nothing to apologize to you for," said the clerk.

Now, we've all been victims of bad customer service in our lives. But until we had a platform—an amplifier—not many people would hear about customer service disasters. With the Web, things are different. Call it revenge of the nerds, if you will. This is what happened to Doubletree.

Most businessmen pound out electronic PowerPoint presentations for meetings, and these businessmen decided to create a Power-Point presentation detailing their experience with Doubletree. It was titled "Yours Is a Very Bad Hotel." The presentation charted the night clerk's career life-cycle curve—peaking at the Doubletree and plummeting thereafter. These two frustrated businessmen used the power of their corporate experience to create charts showing their firm's total 2001 and 2002 hotel expenditures in the Houston area—indicating a missed opportunity for Doubletree of $18,000 worth of annual lodging business. The presentation also compared the odds of death by slipping in a bathtub (1 in 10,455, according to the National Safety Commission) versus the odds of them ever again staying at Doubletree (zero).

They e-mailed the presentation to three people: the manager of the hotel, the front desk manager, and the wife of one of the businessmen. The last page of the presentation asked that they forward the presentation to other friends. Presumably, Doubletree management didn't forward the presentation to their friends.

The single e-mail to the wife resulted in postings of the presentation all over the Web. To date, they have received over four thousand e-mails inquiring if the story was actually true. The story has been picked up in metropolitan newspapers as well as *USA Today*. It's estimated that more than a hundred thousand people have viewed their seventeen-page presentation. And I suspect that many of those hundred thousand now stay away from this chain because of a single disastrous experience, plus the buzz these men put on it.

This painful example of one bad customer-service experience creating something approaching a hundred thousand enemies is a cautionary tale for the Internet age. Word of mouth has power. In this electronic era, negative word of mouth can have the disastrous power of a hurricane.

Guidelines for Policing Your Product

Okay, enough data. Let's talk about an early warning system to police your product.

Maxim 1: Don't Ignore Your Instincts

When you feel in the pit of your stomach that you know the right answer in some situation, pay attention. Especially if you feel that things are beginning to slip—because negative word of mouth could unravel your success faster than you imagine.

Let's assume you've created buzz. Consumers are talking about you, and the media is writing about you. Bravo! But amid all the fast-paced growth, things begin to slip. It happens in every business. Your product may not be what it used to be or what consumers thought it was going to be. Or some of your employees have left and the new crew just doesn't have the same David-vs.-Goliath spirit. Business is sliding.

You're conditioned to think positively, so you reassure yourself it's just a temporary blip, nothing to be concerned about.

Now you discover that customer retention rate is falling, just a little. You know things aren't perfect on the front lines. Yet you ignore your instincts.

Wake up!

Remember that consumers evangelize only for great products. Word-of-mouth marketing works only if you have a great product with an unusual story, or an unusual product that also delivers. You simply won't get sustainable buzz if your product is average.

You and I don't evangelize for the average. You and I don't evangelize for a product that lets us down. In fact, we speak out passionately about a product that strongly disappoints us.

Negative word of mouth can ruin your brand if you don't police your product. It almost ruined Gateway's.

A big piece of any company today has to do with service. Gateway Computers' business relied heavily on the service it provided when you were making your purchase, but also in post-sale whenever you ran into problems.

About ten years ago, Ted Waitt was advised by his bankers and his board to bring in a more professional management team. So he did. They came from AT&T and other Fortune 50 companies. Gateway's new management decided that customer service reps were not efficient. They looked at the profit-and-loss statement, eyed this payroll expense, and decided to slash.

Subsequently, a thirteen-minute efficiency rule was implemented. Gateway customer service reps were reprimanded any time they spent more than thirteen minutes on the phone with customers. If they went over repeatedly, they stood to lose their bonus check. Ted Waitt is a nice guy but he listened to the money men and, for a time, ignored his own instincts.

Now here's something very important. Gateway is a direct-response company, and the only connection with customers is through its customer service reps. Even more important: Fifty percent of its sales came from word-of-mouth referrals, even though Gateway spends over $100 million a year in advertising. What's exquisitely beautiful about this to any manager is that all these new customers were brought in free of any marketing dollars. A lot of people loved their Gateway product and their Gateway service—so much so that they went out of their way to recommend Gateway to their friends. No incremental advertising expense—all free!

But guess what happened? This slick new management team, with all their high-powered résumés, managed to drive word-of-mouth referrals from a high of 50 percent of total sales down to a low of 30 percent of sales.

Professional managers . . . or professional buttheads? Stuff like this really pisses me off! And it also pissed Ted off. He fired the professional buttheads, took the reins of the company, and now word-of-mouth referrals are back up over 50 percent.

So don't ignore your instincts.

Maxim 2: Get Your Leaders on the Front Lines to Police Your Product

Do you know if your product was up to snuff today? How do you know, unless you're policing your product on the front lines?

But hey, that's what management systems are for, right? Delegation? Yes? Well, quite often the person down the line might not have the same passion for the product you do. When you were a kid, did you ever play the game Telephone, where you sat in a circle whispering a phrase to the person next to you, and the last person says the phrase out loud? And then everyone laughs, because it's so very different from the phrase that started out around the circle. As things get passed along, the message can get garbled. Face it, the messages in your company may be getting changed in their travel, just like in the innocent Telephone game.

So the leaders of your organization need to get down to the front lines to ensure the message they whispered (or included in their annual sales meeting speech) is the message that's being heard. And to be sure the messages they're hearing represent what's really going on—especially important in a rapidly changing marketplace.

But, you say, isn't that what management systems are for? If there's a problem, the management system shows it. Here's where the rubber doesn't meet the road.

The number one reason you need leaders on the front lines is because leaders have the power to bypass all the set-in-concrete channels and procedures to remedy the problem. Just as marketing is first about attention, fixing your product is also all about attention. If you can't grab the attention of leaders, then a faulty product and system assumes a life of its own. Quite often it takes someone very powerful to make even the smallest change. And sometimes the smallest change can result in huge impact.

When Arthur Martinez arrived at Sears, one of the first things he did was police the product. As he visited stores, he discovered the obvious. The Sears stores were dark, unattractive, cramped, and filled with boring merchandise.

These stores had been dark, cramped, and filled with boring merchandise for years. Where was the management system to fix it? Wasn't it obvious? Sometimes you need to get your strongest leaders on the front lines. But not just any leaders: leaders with follow-through, who will shift into action when they find a problem that needs fixing. Martinez acted. "It's not useful to be a walk-around manager, to visit stores and hear what needs to be changed, if things don't get changed. Then you're a false prophet," he says.

Martinez created more floor space. He rid the stores of merchandise clutter. He educated employees through a series of what they called town meetings. He built computer information systems that could actually generate information useful to management. He initiated a $4 billion overhaul of the dark, tired stores.

Arthur Martinez policed the product. In five years, he tripled the stock price of Sears.

Some leaders got to the front lines even more frequently, like Steve Jobs. When Apple Computer was launching the Macintosh, he wanted to make sure the first batch was perfect. First impressions count a lot. Jobs went to the Freemont, California, manufacturing plant in December 1983. The product had to get to distributors and into stores by the third week of January, and shipments were already behind.

Before any were shipped, Steve Jobs went to the plant to inspect the computers. Hard drives worked fine, cases looked fine, everything looked fine, except one thing. Jobs held up shipping the Macintosh.

Apple's executive vice president (EVP) in charge of distribution got a phone call . . . not from Jobs but from the plant manager.

"Steve's held up the shipments. They can't go," said the plant manager.

"What!" replied the EVP. "You've got to be kidding me. We're behind schedule already! What's the issue?"

The plant manager responded, "The color."

"You mean the color of the casing?" the executive asked, referring to the molded plastic exterior of the computers.

"No, the color of the box . . . the cardboard box! Jobs says it's too dull . . . not white enough."

"You mean we're behind schedule already . . . and Jobs is holding up shipment of the Mac because he doesn't like the white color of the *cardboard box*?"

"Yup, that's it."

Jobs had left the plant by then.

Later on, the executive vice president discovered Steve Jobs's rationale. The boxes would be stacked on retailers' floors all across America. With new products, first impressions count a lot. The color of the box was too bland and didn't communicate anything sharp or crisp. Jobs held up the shipments and new boxes had to be printed.

At first, the executive vice president was baffled—and a little peeved. Dealers were breathing down his neck, asking "Where the hell is the product?" The company had the product, but not the right colored box.

Ultimately, he recognized that Jobs was right. First impressions do count a lot for a new product. The decision to hold up the product was the right one.

Do you know anyone today who would have the guts to delay shipment of a much awaited new product . . . over the color of a box? Chances are nobody else at Apple would have had the guts. Not even the executive vice president. But small details can have a huge impact.

Getting a leader on the front lines gives you a high degree of assurance that the product you designed is the same product getting to the final customer.

Furthermore, when workers find out that leaders are paying attention to the details of the product, then *everyone* pays more attention to the details. I'll wager that after Jobs held up the Mac shipment, word of his action spread to every employee within twenty-four hours, by internal word of mouth. Who wouldn't want to work for a company with a leader like that—one with guts.

Maxim 3: Survey, Survey, Survey—but Use Only Two Questions

Almost every customer satisfaction survey I've seen or heard of falls short.

The former CEO of KFC once made a comment that has stayed with me for fifteen years. He said, "Sometimes we can be very precise, but inaccurate." With 99 percent of surveys, this is an appropriate description.

Surveying is good in any form, informal or formal. It shows intent; it shows you seek improvement and you seek information. You're ahead of the game. But chances are if you're surveying employees, distributors, and customers formally, you're asking too many questions and probably the wrong ones.

I can save you lots of money and lots of time.

Throw out every question except for two. All other questions are meaningless data dung.

The first question: How did you first hear about us? This tracks word-of-mouth percentage and marketing effectiveness.

The second and perhaps most important question: Would you go out of your way to recommend our product to a friend?

Notice the deliberate wording. It doesn't simply ask, "Would you recommend to a friend?" But rather, would you *go out of your way* to recommend to a friend. A subtle but important distinction. A distinction measuring customer evangelism—or buzz.

Every other question is worthless, wasting your money and time. "Overall experience"—data dung. "Overall quality"—data dung.

What "overall quality" misses is the discovery of the buzz factor for your product. If you measure overall quality, that tells you zero about the most important ingredient for getting buzz— whether your customers will evangelize for you. It's one thing to have an average product that does an okay sort of job, but if you have a product you're proud of and expect customers to be highly satisfied with, then you have the right to hope for word-of-mouth buzz. If customers won't evangelize for you, you won't get buzz and take off.

To break out and get buzz, you need to measure if your customers are evangelizing for you. Do they go out of their way to talk about you? If they do—great. Now keep on surveying to make sure you don't lose it and reach a point where, for some reason, they are no longer evangelizing for you.

Measure "overall quality" and you're stuck in the world of average. But measure evangelism, and you'll be on the road to getting buzz. Remember the survey rule of two questions.

Maxim 4: Motivate Your Employees . . . with Buzz!

Great employees tremendously affect your sales and profits. According to the author Bill Fromm and Jim Heskitt of the Harvard Business School, companies that distinguish themselves by the way they hire, train, and treat their employees experience growth rates from 60 to 300 percent higher than their competitors. They also experience a return on assets from 150 to 300 percent higher than their competitors. One and a half to three times the return on assets!

Guess what? Great employees save you marketing dollars, and great employees accelerate growth. Unhappy employees won't evangelize for you. Average employees won't help you slay Goliath.

What's the number one thing that employees want (besides more money)? They want communication! And what's the best way to communicate to people? It's what we've been talking about throughout this book: word-of-mouth buzz.

Communicate to your employees through a means that resonates with them, that starts conversations and proliferates. You can do this using the same approach we've been talking about in this entire book. Employees, just like consumers, talk about:

The taboo
The unusual
The outrageous
The hilarious
The remarkable
Secrets (both kept and revealed)

Believe it or not, you don't want to focus your word of mouth on profits. You don't want employees talking about stock valuations. "Heresy," you say! Of course you want people talking about profits and stock—that's what business is all about!

But I have another take on this subject. Business is about making products, getting customers to buy them, and getting customers to buy them again. Profits are a result of the product.

Don't pump your people up about sales goals and profit goals (though that's not to say you don't measure people on metrics). Guess what? Sales goals and profit goals are boring. Do you really think your employees will talk to their friends about the fact that you hit this quarter's goal? Employees talk about the same thing that consumers talk about: the unusual, the outrageous, the taboo, the hilarious, the remarkable, and . . . especially about secrets.

Another word for buzz in the workplace is the *grapevine.* The grapevine is the most powerful and efficient form of communication within any company. Use it to your advantage.

Employees don't talk about how many widgets they produced this month. Saturn employees talk about how their company spent $3,000 to fly a technician to Alaska to repair a $300 part. Employees talk about how the CEO works the floor every two weeks. Employees talk about how the board of directors visited fifty-seven stores last year . . . and how a few members of the board visited their store or office.

They talk about the sales associate at Nordstrom who took back a tire for a refund, even though Nordstrom doesn't sell tires.

Employees at Gateway talk about how they can "Win Ted's Paycheck" (CEO Ted Waitt's $10,000 paycheck) in a competition on ideas for improving customer service or reducing costs. That's what employees talk about—the unusual!

Eventually, every business hits a bump in the road. If you pump your employees with financial metric propaganda as your buzz, it will demotivate people when you hit that bump in the road and your stock stalls. It does the exact opposite of what you need, just when you need it most.

You've got to give your employees a story they can get excited about and tell to their friends. You've got to pump them with stories of unusual customer service, outrageous marketing, employees rewarded with remarkable trips to Hawaii just for doing their everyday job. This transcends profit propaganda and gives employees something they can evangelize about. When you hit that financial bump in the road (and you will), morale built on buzz won't sink with the stock price.

Remember: The grapevine is the most powerful form of communication in your company. When you understand what generates word-of-mouth buzz, you can communicate and resonate with your organization faster. Give them something to talk about.

If you've had a great experience with a business, chances are it's because of its employees, not its marketing. I had a fantastic experience with AT&T Small Business Service—not because of any marketing, not because of any other reason most businesspeople might guess, but all because a woman named Pat S. in the toll-free service group went beyond the call of duty, solved my problem, and wowed me. In this case, AT&T's product is service . . . they delivered 110 percent service and now I dare anyone to find a better telephone company. (And in case you didn't notice, that was an example of a happy customer evangelizing for a company and a product, unasked.)

The likelihood of my staying with the company and evangelizing for them has everything to do with the employees who make the product, sell the product, and service the product.

Buzz Leadership Pays

If you had a choice of working for a conventional company versus a company that encourages creativity and generates word-of-mouth buzz, which company would you want to work for?

Today, competitive advantage is often defined by your employees, their innovations, and their ability to turn ideas into reality. A buzz culture can attract and retain forward thinkers.

Using the secrets of buzzmarketing to get consumers evangelizing about your brand begins with getting employees to evangelize about your brand. Getting your employees to evangelize about your brand is more important. After all, if your employees aren't evangelizing for you . . . do you think consumers will? When surveying your own employees (and you should), ask them if they would go out of their way to recommend your product to a friend. Anything less than 100 percent signals trouble.

Remember those statistics: Companies that distinguish themselves by the way they hire, train, and treat their employees experience growth rates from 60 to 300 percent higher than their competitors and experience a return on assets from 150 to 300 percent higher than their competitors. Using the secrets of buzzmarketing with your employees saves you marketing dollars, and accelerates your growth.

Policing your product, delivering a great product, and using the secrets of buzz with your employees—these are the foundations of buzz, and this is the architecture of companies that get buzz and break away from the pack.

Statisticians call them anomalies; consumers call them successful. Consultants call them cash cows; academics call them brand leaders. They know buzz, they get buzz.

Afterword

In the past, buzzmarketing was perceived as a serendipitous happening. But now, with the studies cited earlier showing that word of mouth is ten times more effective than TV or print, advertisers are starting to take notice.

You can continue searching for solutions along the current path of marketing, but it's a path that most experts admit is in turmoil. Companies like Pepsi have tried throwing money at the problem, and then succeeded by throwing unconventional smarts instead.

Buzzmarketing is about knowing, living, and breathing the Six Secrets. It's about getting consumers to talk about your brand, and getting the media to write about your brand.

Buzzmarketing is a structured practice of out-thinking instead of out-spending.

Business Week notes "even the most blue chip marketers—right up to Ford and Procter & Gamble—are trying their hand at buzz." Even the likes of McKinsey & Company are studying it more and more—calling for companies "to refocus their marketing lenses on consumer-to-consumer communications—be they verbal, visual, or digital. That's where buzz is born."

The Six Secrets of Buzzmarketing

Buzzmarketing is anything but happenstance. It isn't random. It isn't serendipitous. If you market your business every day by tapping into the structure of the Six Secrets, you will experience breakaway growth.

It's not that hard if you practice the Six Secrets.

1. Push the Six Buttons of Buzz

There's no textbook teaching you that word of mouth is the most powerful form of marketing on earth. Getting people talking about your brand will grow your brand exponentially. But the key to understanding the nature of word-of-mouth marketing is giving people a ready-made story to talk about. Sing it with me and Bonnie Raitt: "Let's give 'em something to talk about!" Whether it's the taboo, or the outrageous, or one of the others—push any one of six buttons, and you'll start conversations.

2. Capture Media

The media can shape your image and pour gasoline on your buzz . . . just ask Ben & Jerry's, or John McEnroe. The secret isn't under lock and key—just understand America's five most frequently written news stories.

3. Advertise for Attention
(Screw convention . . . it's all about attention)

Educate, inform, persuade—wake up people, this ain't it! Unless you can capture attention, the conventional rules of advertising are just about over. Reinvent media or create media, like Allen Odell with Burma Shave in 1925. Get heard or follow the herd.

4. Climb Buzz Everest

Remember how Don Price was forced to manage Rit dye without advertising, turning around a brand that was deader than a doornail. In the process, he created America's tie-dye phenomenon. What's your Buzz Everest?

5. Discover Creativity

Whether it's Henry Kissinger or Jimmy Johnson, you've got to demand the very best to get the very best. Be careful what you wish for . . . a kick-ass idea might make you uncomfortable. Do you have the courage? The choice is yours: Out-think your competition or out-spend them.

6. Police Your Product

Negative buzz can unravel all your efforts in a heartbeat. Let your product guard down, and the numbers can be against you by 10,000 to 23. Steve Jobs was a fanatical leader who policed his product and had the guts to hold up shipment of an already overdue Macintosh. But where does buzz really begin? It begins at home: If you want consumers to evangelize about your product, start with your employees and give them something to talk about!

Are You Ready?

The secrets of buzz are logical. The hardest part of buzz is generating the creative idea that plugs into the framework. Coming up with an idea to rename a town is one thing—but actually *doing it* is entirely different. It takes courage, commitment, faith, and effort.

Buzz is not an off-the shelf proposition. Every idea begins with a clean slate. Taking the path less traveled is never without risk and never easy. But it will make all the difference.

Are you ready?

acknowledgments

Josh Kopelman for believing in me. Jim Kilberg for all he's done for me. My literary agents Richard Pine and Matthew Guma for their faith, keen insight, and hard work. Adrian Zackheim for his wonderful sixth sense. Editor Stephanie Land, Associate Editor Megan Casey, and PR gurus Will Weisser and Allison Sweet for all their hard work and amazing skill. John and Libby Hughes for their help and love.

Many thanks to those for their kind and insightful endorsements of *Buzzmarketing:* Ben Cohen, cofounder of Ben & Jerry's Ice Cream and president of TrueMajority.org; Steve Forbes at *Forbes* magazine; Warren Phillips, former editor of the *Wall Street Journal* and CEO of Dow Jones; author Stan Rapp; and Brian Swette, former chief marketing officer at Pepsi and former chief operating officer at eBay.

And many more who helped contribute to *Buzzmarketing:* Bill Aho at ClearPlay; Bill Backer; Chip Benson; Kerri Benson; Marc Berkowitz; Margaret Block at Kleiner Perkins; Lisa Bowen at the Salt Lake *Deseret Morning News;* David Buckley in Little Silver, New Jersey; Bill Cobb at eBay; Alan Cohen; Jim Corboy at Northwestern University's Kellogg School of Management; Bob Cringely; Pat Croce; Jim Davie at Davie-Brown; Dave Dececco at Pepsi; Frank Delano; Laura Dellapenna at Deutsch; Nick Denton at Gawker; Irving Der at Disney Radio; Dan Dymtrow at ReignDeer Entertainment; Erwin Ephron; Ryan Farley at BuddyGopher.com; Professor William Finnie at Washington University; Chris Fralic at eBay; Bill Fromm at Barkley Evergreen; Cecile Frot-Coutaz at Fremantle Media; Lance Funston at TelamericaMedia; Jim Galbraith at Columbia University Library; Earl Galleher; A. J. Gil, *American Idol* singer; Nick Gray at BuddyGopher.com; Jeff Greenfield at WorldClassMedia. com; Gabriel Griego at Game Ready; all my friends in Halfway, Oregon, and Pine Valley; Mark Harrington; Eliza Heiman at ReignDeer Entertainment; Jeff Hicks at Crispin Porter + Bogusky; Eric Hirshberg at Deutsch; Julie Hoffman at Mini; Nancy Hubbell at Toyota; Tom Huestis; Vickie Huestis; Matt Jarman at ClearPlay; Jason Jennings at Jennings Solutions; Matt Jesson; Robin Jones at Disney Radio; Kristin Keyes; Sandy King at Fremantle Media; AnnaMarie Kino at the World Advertising Research Center; Jack Kraushaar; Rob Kulat; Floyd Kvamme at Kleiner Perkins; Chico Lager; Ho Sing Lee; Bob Lenz; Richard Leung; Anna Manzano at Fremantle Media; Kerri Martin at Mini; Walter (Chip) Mead; Andy Merz; Chris Miller; Sarah Mollo-Christensen; Brad Moses; Steve Norcia; Eric Nuzum at NPR; Tom Oliver at Game Ready; Joe McCann; Mike McCarthy at *USA Today;* Jay Peichel; Danielle Perry at AT&T; Duane Peterson at TrueMajority.org; Alan Pottasch; Don Price; Pete Reader; Jacqueline Reid at Duke University's Hartman Center; Tom Robinson in Seattle; Jamie Rosen at Comet; Larry Rudolph at ReignDeer Entertainment; Dell Schanze at Totally Awesome Computers; Clint Schmidt; Brad Shaw at Gateway; Darren Shuster; Eli Silberman; Geoff Slick at SlickIdeasDesign.com; Ben Slingerland; Adam Solomon at Screensavers.com; Steve Tart; Sonia Taylor; Pat Tessman; Professor Bob Thompson; Nate Tyler at Google; Professor Patti Williams at the Wharton School of Business (who probably never knew her invitation to speak spawned this book); and Phyllis Wasserman.

Finally, thanks to Bill Simon for his efforts in helping to shape the manuscript and fine tune the text. A best-selling author in his own right, Bill made a contribution beyond measure.

notes

Chapter 1: Evading the Stampede

Page

2 **Ten times more effective:** Euro RSCG Worldwide, "Wired & Wireless: High-Tech Capitals Now and Next." http://www.eurorscg.com/press/pop .asp?id=96.

4 **More than twenty-three thousand new products:** Mintel Global New Products Database, Press Center, http://www.gnpd.com/uk/gnpd/about/ press.htm.

Chapter 2: Renaming a Town

18 **"Moving Ideas into Action":** Rosabeth Moss Canter, "Moving Ideas into Action: Mastering the Art of Change" (study, Harvard Business School, 1987).

21 **The story was scheduled to run:** Sam Howe Verhovek, "City Weighs Price of Its Good Name," *New York Times,* January 11, 2000.

Chapter 3: The First Secret—Push the Six Buttons of Buzz

25 **audio stimulus stays with you longer:** Taylor Nelson Sofres, "Use and Effectiveness of Musical Cues in Advertising," http://www.mcvaymedia.com/ salespromo/musicalcues.htm#_ftn2.

25 **ten times more effective:** Euro RSCG Worldwide, "Wired & Wireless.

30 **sales were higher with Whipple:** Luke Sullivan, *"Hey Whipple, Squeeze This." A Guide to Creating Great Ads* (New York: John Wiley & Sons, 1998).

38 **three to ten times higher sales:** George Silverman, *The Secrets of Word of Mouth Marketing: How to Trigger Exponential Sales Through Runaway World of Mouth* (New York: AMACOM, 2001).

38 **a ten-times impact:** George Lois, *What's the Big Idea? How to Win with Outrageous Ideas (That Sell!)* (New York: Plume, 1991).

Chapter 4: Miller Lite: A Brand Before Its Time

40 **A Brand Before Its Time:** Bill Backer (McCann-Erickson), Eli Silberman, Steve Tart, and Steve Norcino (McCann-Erickson), in discussion with the author, summer and fall, 2002.

Chapter 5: Starting Up from Scratch—Green for Greenfield

61 **Dahv:** For more information on Dr. Jeff's protégée, Dahv, visit www. Dahv.com.

Chapter 6: *American Idol*

63 **"get noticed and talked about":** Mike Darnell, interview in *Adrants,* February, 2003, http://www.adrants.com/2003/02/mike-darnell-man-behind-reality-tvs.php.

65 **"[*American Idol*] is to *Star Search*":** Todd Leopold, "Kelly is crowned 'American Idol,'" CNN.com, September 5, 2002, http://archives.cnn.com/2002/SHOWBIZ/TV/09/05/american.idol.

66 **more than a hundred live appearances:** Marc Gunther, "The MVP of Late Night," *Fortune,* February 10, 2004, http://www.fortune.com/fortune/ceo/articles/0,15114,588972,00.html.

73 **overall U.S. text message volume:** Catharine P. Taylor, "Time to Send a Message," *Brandweek,* July 12, 2004, http://www.brandweek.com/brandweek/search/article_display.jsp?rnu_content_id=1000574697.

Chapter 7: The Second Secret—Capture Media

82 **Kiwi Airlines was now taking off:** Kiwi's later demise stemmed not from inadequate sales growth, but from a poor economic operating model.

83 **Ben & Jerry's total sales:** Fred "Chico" Lager, *The Inside Scoop* (New York: Crown, 1994).

93 **"pop culture pulse taker":** Michael T. Jarvis, "The Screensaver as Pulse Taker," *Los Angeles Times,* March 14, 2004, E3.

Chapter 8: Apple Mac Attack: What Few Know

Parts of this chapter are based on an interview with Floyd Kvamme, Apple Computer's executive vice president of marketing and sales during this period, in discussion with the author, spring 2003.

102 **"the battle for market supremacy":** *Business Week,* "Personal Computers: and the Winner Is IBM," October 3, 1983, 72.

Chapter 10: The Third Secret—Advertise for Attention

120 **more than a thousand:** Jonathan Bond, Richard Kirshenbaum, *Under the Radar: Talking to Today's Cynical Consumer* (New York: John Wiley & Sons, 1998).

121 **71 percent of people:** eBrain Market Research, "TiVo Study," Consumer Electronics Association, April 2000, http://www.ebrain.com.

121 **On the relationship between memory and magazine thickness:** Erwin Ephron, conversation with author, February 2002.

121 **the *more* advertising in a given medium:** Al Ries and Laura Ries, *The Fall of Advertising and the Rise of PR* (New York: HarperCollins, 2002).

123 **"Our 'rules' [of advertising]":** Ken Sacharin, *Attention! How to Interrupt, Yell, Whisper, and Touch Customers* (New York: Wiley, 2000).

123 **"Advertisers have many new choices":** Lauren Rich Fine, "Adnotes," *Wall Street Journal,* June 9, 2004.

124 **you'll produce a greater response:** Erwin Ephron, "Media Mix: The New Media Planning Is About Picking Combinations of Media," *Advertising Age,* February 28, 2000.

124 **"the 30 second commercial":** *Fortune,* April 1, 2001.

124 **"It's not rampant":** Ephron, "Media Mix."

124 **"TV advertising":** Brian Steinberg, "Advert Mailbox," *Wall Street Journal,* June 9, 2004.

131 **96 percent:** Study of 584 people surveyed at a Philadelphia suburban Chinese food restaurant. Consumers asked to name up to six vodka brands. Control period with no vodka ad on back of fortune in January 2003. Test period with vodka ad on back of fortune in February 2003.

132 **32 million people a month:** Buzzmarketing Web site, FortuneCookie Ads.com, http://www.buzzmedia.com/fortunecookieads.

132 **39 percent:** Study of 584 people surveyed at a Philadelphia suburban Chinese food restaurant. Consumers asked to name up to six vodka brands. Control period with no vodka ad on back of fortune in January 2003. Test period with vodka ad on back of fortune in February 2003.

134 **BuddyGopher:** Nick Gray and Ryan Farley; www.buddygopher.com.

139 **five times longer:** Roy H. Williams, *Secret Formulas of the Wizard of Ads* (Staten Island: Bard Press, 1999).

141 **"the most coveted commodity of all":** Thomas Weber "Web Marketers Turn Advertising on Its Head," *Wall Street Journal,* November 1, 1999. http://exxodus.webhostme.com/code/wsjournalA.asp.

Chapter 11: Building Britney Buzz

153 **"world's most powerful celebrity":** "Celebrity 100 List," *Forbes,* June 2002.

Chapter 12: The Fourth Secret—Climb Buzz Everest

164 **"Failure is our most important product":** James C. Collins and Jerry I. Porras, *Built to Last: Successful Habits of Visionary Companies* (New York: HarperCollins, 2002).

Chapter 13: War of the Colas: A Story Behind the Story

165 Material in this chapter is based on interviews with Pete Reader, Brad Moses, Alan Pottasch, Joe McCann, and Jim Davie in discussion with the author, fall 2002.

165 **Pepsi would be an insignificant factor:** Roger Enrico, *The Other Guy Blinked: How Pepsi Won the Cola Wars* (New York: Bantam Books, 1986).

173 **495 billion cases:** Case volume according to the Beverage Industry Manual, 1972 vs. 1985. Beverage Industry Annual Manual (New York: Magazines for Industry and Business, 1985).

173 **from 37 to 10 percent:** Ibid.

Chapter 14: The Fifth Secret—Discover Creativity

174 **85 percent:** Lois, *What's the Big Idea?*

174 **"advertisers get the creative they deserve":** Enrico, *The Other Guy Blinked.*

175 **"That's the responsibility of every leader":** Ibid.

176 **"when an ad promises to cause a stir":** John Philip Jones, "The Mismanagement of Advertising," *Harvard Business Review,* January–February 2000.

177 **a see-more:** Anthony Parinello, *Selling to VITO (The Very Important Top Officer)* (Avon, MA: Adams Media, 1999).

178 **"Enough with strategies":** Frank Delano, *Brand Slam: The Ultimate Hit in the Game of Marketing* (New York: Lebhar-Friedman Books, 2001).

179 **"You can't learn a damned thing":** Enrico, *The Other Guy Blinked.*

182 **His estimate was one in twenty:** Erwin Ephron, "Why Consolidate Media: The Best Reason Is Better Advertising," December 1996, http://www.ephrononmedia.com/index.asp.

183 **"The one-upmanship factor":** Bob Latchky, interview in *Ad Age,* May 29, 2000, http://www.ephrononmedia.com/index.asp.

183 **Crispin Porter + Bogusky:** This section is based on an interview with Jeff Hicks (president, Crispin Porter + Bogusky), in discussion with author, summer 2002.

Chapter 15: Mustang Bang

196 **Walter Mead:** Walter Mead (chief creative director of J. Walter Thompson), in discussion with the author, fall 2002.

Chapter 16: The Sixth Secret—Police Your Product

206 **the first rule of marketing:** Victor Kiam, quoted in Adam Morgan, *Eating the Big Fish: How Challenger Brands Can Compete Against Brand Leaders* (New York: John Wiley & Sons, 1999).

208 **VW had to offer $3,000 incentives:** David Kiley, "Quality-control Guru Tackles VW Problems," *USA Today,* May 12, 2004.

208 **100,000 people were chatting about it:** Ibid.

209 **The impact of 23 complaining customers:** Roy H. Williams, *Secret Formulas of the Wizard of Ads* (Austin, Texas: Bard Press, 1999).

213 **thirteen-minute efficiency rule:** Katrina Booker, "I Built This Company, I Can Save It," *Fortune,* April 31, 2001, 94.

215 **"It's not useful":** Arthur Martinez, "I Do Preach Serendipity," *Business Week,* November 1, 2001.

219 **growth rates from 60 to 300 percent higher:** Bill Fromm, *The Ten Commandments of Business—and How to Break Them: Secrets for Improving Employee Morale, Enhancing Customer Service, Increasing Company Profit* (New York: Putnam, 1991).

Afterword

223 **"even the most blue chip marketers":** Gerry Khermouch and Jeff Green, "Buzz Marketing," *Business Week,* July 30, 2001.

223 **"That's where buzz is born":** Renee Dye, "The Buzz on Buzz," *Harvard Business Review,* November–December, 2000.

Index